Wealth Exposed

Founded in 1807, John Wiley & Sons is the oldest independent publishing company in the United States. With offices in North America, Europe, Australia and Asia, Wiley is globally committed to developing and marketing print and electronic products and services for our customers' professional and personal knowledge and understanding.

The Wiley Finance series contains books written specifically for finance and investment professionals as well as sophisticated individual investors and their financial advisors. Book topics range from portfolio management to e-commerce, risk management, financial engineering, valuation and financial instrument analysis, as well as much more.

For a list of available titles, visit our website at www.WileyFinance.com.

Wealth Exposed

Insurance Planning for High Net Worth Individuals and Their Advisors

Brian G. Flood, CPCU, ARM

WILEY

For my wife, Regina, whose love and support provides the foundation as our dreams are pursued.

My children, Francesca, Andrew, and Peter John (PJ), who remind me each day of the joy of being a dad. Dream big and great things will happen!

My late father, Gerard, who taught me the insurance business and the importance of integrity.

My mother, always excited to hear my dreams and ambitions, no matter how outrageous, encouraging all the way to always reach for the stars.

Terry, my brother and business partner. A great pilot, captain, and navigator in business, in the air, and on the seas.

Contents

Introduction

May you live in interesting times.

—Ancient proverb

These are, indeed, interesting times for people of wealth, but perhaps not in the way you would like to think. I had always thought this ancient proverb to be a blessing that wishes the gift of wisdom for someone. However, it was recently explained to me that it is actually a curse—*a less-noble wish for an experience of upheaval and anxiety*. While I wouldn't necessarily wish that upon anybody, the adage turns out to be appropriately prophetic for what has transpired over the last several years in the lives of people who have attained higher levels of wealth.

As anyone would have expected, the extraordinary convergence of a housing and stock market crash, a credit crisis, a recession, and years of irresponsible fiscal management of our government has taken a severe toll on the American psyche. As if suffering significant losses of net worth during the extended crisis wasn't enough, the wealthy have become ground-zero in the politically inspired tumult that spawned the "Occupy Wall Street" movement and ignited a heated election-year debate over their "fair share."

In this new theater of class war, people who would otherwise desire to live quiet, productive, and often charitable lives now find themselves targeted by government redistributionists and resented by the "99 Percent." But, if recent trends are any indication, the wealthy may have bigger worries than mere taxes and scorn. As the growing income disparity continues to widen the divide between the so-called "haves" and "have-nots," the wealthy now face a much higher risk of becoming the target of "citizen redistributionists"—those seeking their "fair share" through an accommodating justice system.

We're all familiar with the general theme: A group of teenage boys stage a harmless prank that goes bad, injuring an unsuspecting boy. Three of the boys, sons of local manufacturing workers, receive nothing more than a verbal lashing and a school suspension, while the fourth, the son of a high-profile CEO, becomes the subject of major lawsuit. Follow the money. Fortunately, the injured boy just suffered a broken collar bone and the trauma of humiliation; so the court merely awards $100,000 in damages. Had the prank gone really bad, resulting in a brain injury or death, the damages would have rocketed into the tens of millions of dollars. It always comes down to a capricious twist of fate that could have life-changing consequences.

In a society already deemed the most litigious in the world, the stakes for people with assets are increasing at an alarming rate; yet, many high net worth individuals remain dangerously unprepared. As you might expect from a financially astute segment of the population, it's not necessarily from a lack of awareness of the risks; rather, it is generally from a drastic underestimation of their liabilities and a lack of understanding of how to effectively use personal risk management strategies and insurance to protect themselves and their assets.

THE CHALLENGES OF WEALTH AND THE NEXT LEVEL

Property, casualty, and liability coverage is difficult for most people to understand at any level; but when you spend your life building wealth, and, as a byproduct, adding multiple layers of liability, it can become overwhelmingly complex at the next level. The problem for people who ascend to the next level of wealth is that they continue to rely on insurance coverage designed for their simpler, past lives. Several pieces of real estate, a few staff hires, and a couple of new luxury cars later, and their patchwork of mass-market insurance policies provides less protection than an umbrella in a cyclone.

At the other end of the spectrum are those who do expect to pay more for higher-end coverage, but, through a piecemeal approach to addressing their protection needs, they wind up overinsuring for smaller losses, or shelling out more for premiums than they should. In reviewing the insurance policies of wealthy individuals, I constantly come across exceedingly high deductibles on small risks, or I find a complete lack of policy coordination, both of which result in highly inefficient pricing, not to mention the failure to take advantage of significant discounts.

Underestimating risk or using inefficient solutions is likely to occur when people climbing the wealth ladder outgrow the capacity of their original property-casualty agent, who may not have access to the specialized risk management solutions needed at the next level. For the same reason why a high net worth investor wouldn't seek off-the-shelf investment advice from a stockbroker, people with substantial assets to protect shouldn't rely on mass market solutions to navigate the liability minefield. Perhaps the more appropriate analogy is the Maserati owner who takes his car to a Volkswagen mechanic. You don't do it because, although he may be a great mechanic, he would quickly hit his ceiling of competence, which is well below what would be required.

In each of these circumstances, the level of complexity—be it managing a $2 million investment portfolio, protecting $20 million of assets, or keeping the most technologically advanced car precisely tuned—far surpasses both the competence level and the resource capacity of the provider to understand it, let alone provide the proper solutions.

There are those who don't know their limitations, but they earnestly try to do what they think is best for the client; there are also those who know that they don't know and yet are willing to offer solutions they know to be inadequate. Both present a danger to high net worth individuals who simply don't know what they need to know, and who continue to treat insurance coverage as a commodity.

With the vast majority of wealth climbers still being served by mass-market carriers, there remains a severe knowledge gap that will continue to cost them billions of dollars a year in losses. While an increasing number of people are awakening to the deficiency in their coverage, it's not until they are on the business end of lawsuit or learn that their property loss far exceeds their current coverage that many finally seek expert guidance. And, of course, at that point it's too late. But their consolation is that the likelihood of another high-stakes occurrence is probable for people of wealth, so it can never be too late to seek the proper guidance.

WHY *WEALTH EXPOSED* NEEDED TO BE WRITTEN

We have entered an extraordinary period when "winning by not losing" is of paramount importance. That has become true of investment management in a much more volatile market. And it is becoming even more critical in risk management at a time when our litigious society grows more restless in the pursuit of its fair share. While it is in the best interest of high net worth individuals to seek the guidance of a well-qualified, objective professional in both of these disciplines, it is also to their advantage to at least become conversant in the language so they are aware of what they don't know.

Having worked extensively with high net worth clients for more than 20 years, I can appreciate the extraordinary sacrifices they make in climbing the ladder of success. These sacrifices include the cost of navigating the complexities of a comprehensive financial plan and managing their ever-increasing risks.

I have observed that successful people are particularly disadvantaged when it comes to acquiring the essential knowledge needed to protect what they have. Most are so deeply involved in their business or in pursuing the expanding body of knowledge required to keep on top of their professions that they have little time to even think about the perils that lurk about them.

Accordingly, I have made no attempt to create a "deep-in-the-weeds" textbook-style resource that only insurance professionals, lawyers, and financial advisors could appreciate. Rather, this book is intended to demystify the world of risk management and provide a practical guide for preoccupied, successful people to familiarize themselves with the risks they face, as well as the insurance solutions designed specifically for the high net worth individual. At a minimum, this is what you need to become more fully engaged when you do sit down with a qualified, objective insurance professional. And this will also help you tell the good ones from the bad ones.

Essentially, I wrote the book that I have long searched for but could never find as recommended reading for my own clients, who appreciate clarity without all of the jargon, and who want to be better prepared when they discuss their protection needs with their advisors.

HOW TO USE THIS BOOK

While *Wealth Exposed* does require at least a rudimentary understanding of how insurance works, the more advanced concepts presented are written in clear and concise language to facilitate an easy and, I hope, an engaging learning experience.

Equally important, this book is written in the context of the high net worth lifestyle, replete with concepts, case studies, and tips specific to your unique needs. The detailed table of contents is your compass, pointing you to your most pressing needs, or you can simply follow the clearly marked path of concepts that are lined with all of the key elements of an integrated, comprehensive risk management plan.

The information contained in this book is for informational purposes only and is not to be construed as advice. A qualified, independent personal lines insurance specialist should always be consulted before making any decision regarding your personal risk management plan.

The characters and cases used in the book are based on actual client situations but their names and specific details have been altered to protect their privacy.

Please be sure to visit www.wealth-exposed.com to find additional Personal Risk Management resources.

Wealth Exposed

CHAPTER 1

Welcome! You Are at the Next Level

Who doesn't love an inspiring "rags-to-riches" story? We're fascinated when we learn about a Harvard dropout who fails in his first venture but goes on to build one of the most successful computer software companies ever. We're enamored with the young man who sold Coke bottles to stay in school and ate charity meals before collaborating with another young man in his parents' garage to create the world's first personal computer. His creation ultimately built the world's most valuable company in terms of market capitalization.

Why do we love these stories? Because many of us start off with nothing and aspire to make a success of our lives. They help us believe that anything is possible. But, some people find it's hard to imagine rich and famous people ever struggling for money. While all success stories are not of the rags-to-riches variety, what is lost on those with that mindset is that the vast majority of successful people began their careers from the same hole in which we all start. It's difficult for the average person to fully gauge, let alone appreciate, the time and money commitment that goes into building a successful business or career.

A REAL-WORLD SUCCESS STORY

I could blindly pick from the files of my high net worth clients and find story after story of how they began their climb in settings familiar to most people. One in particular, I'll call John, is the founder of a very successful multinational company with a thousand employees. But John struggled for a long time before he made his first dollar of profit. Married right out of college, he and his wife started a family early, and they both worked at various jobs just to maintain a modest lifestyle while he pursued his entrepreneurial passion.

It was only after he had sunk every dime he had into his venture, paying his employees while denying himself a salary, that it began to generate the kind of profits that could support his modest lifestyle. Ten years later, he took his company public, and his paper net worth rocketed to $100 million. His family now enjoys a wealthy lifestyle. They live in a mansion on 10 acres in upper New York State, with horses, a small vineyard, and a staff of seven. As is typical of many of my wealthy clients, John remains the same decent and grounded person he was when he lived in a two-bedroom apartment 20 years ago.

His will probably never be the rags-to-riches story people will talk about, but John should be an example for anyone who finds himself on the path to success and riches. You see, John didn't just suddenly wake up one day to find he was a multimillionaire (although that does happen—lottery winners, pro athletes, instant-celebrity performers, etc.—but that's a different story). He did a lot of planning along the way to get it right.

As the son of very prudent parents who diligently saved their money for his college education, John believed in planning. He also believed in surrounding himself with competent advisors. Even before his business took off, he had devoted time and energy to develop a financial blueprint for his family. A lot would change in his financial life along the way, but he understood the value of staying engaged in planning so he could feel in control of his financial future.

In addition to financial planning, John sought the advice of legal professionals specializing in business. As his business grew, he surrounded himself with business experts who coached and mentored him. John continued to pursue educational opportunities to further his personal and business development (including a Dale Carnegie course at the age of 55). And he eventually formed a team of advisors who would coordinate all of the above with a long-term investment strategy. He accomplished all of this while he spent an inordinate amount of time working on his business. He also gave back to his community with generous amounts of his time and money.

The obvious point here is John's road to success was not only paved with challenges, it was built with many pieces and a significant investment before he got to the next level. There was just one piece missing, and for someone in John's position its absence had the potential to take almost everything he had worked for away from him. As he would later learn, the missing piece of the puzzle was a comprehensive personal risk management strategy.

Through all of the years of building his business and climbing the wealth ladder, John continued his relationship with his original property and casualty agent. In fact, he was same agent his father had used more than 30 years ago. John did update his homeowners insurance on a new house he bought; he even bought a million-dollar umbrella policy as his attorney advised. In all, John's agent helped him to address most of his personal risks, but it was done incrementally through a hodgepodge of insurance policies.

As John's wealth grew, so did his risk exposure. Nothing was done to assess the risks or determine the true extent of his exposure. John spent most of his time working on his business, which, as you might expect, was pretty well insured against business liabilities. So, as you also might expect, he had little time to consider the personal exposure he was amassing, or, if he did, he felt he had sufficient protection through his existing policies. It wasn't that John wasn't thorough in his planning, it's just that he and his advisors did not understand the personal risk management needs of high net worth individuals.

A Riches-to-Rags Story?

Flash forward to September 2006, when John and his family moved into their new home, a beautiful, expansive colonial replete with a guesthouse and another two-story house to be used as quarters for his growing staff. This was before he took his company public. Still, through a sound investment plan, and the sale of a part of his business to a private equity firm, John's net worth had grown to $30,000,000, half of which resided in his equity share of the company.

While John and his family were out of town, the housekeeper, Shauna, invited her 10-year-old niece to spend a few days with her. This was a clear violation of John's rules. The staff quarters were big enough so the temporary addition of little girl would not impose on anyone. Shauna left her niece to play in the staff quarters while she went to the main house to clean. When she went back an hour later to check on her niece, she found her lying in a lifeless heap on the ground outside the quarters, her head bloodied. Looking up, Shauna saw the splintered wood that had been the railing of the second floor widow's walk. She called 911, and the paramedics arrived 20 minutes later.

Shauna's niece suffered severe injuries to her brain. She would be unable to lead a normal life, and she would require lifetime, round-the-clock nursing care. A jury awarded the girl's family $25 million dollars—$5 million for pain and suffering and $20 million for medical care—far more than was covered by John's $1.3 million personal liability coverage from his homeowners and umbrella liability policies. John was forced to liquidate his equity in the company to pay the judgment. He didn't lose everything, but his life would change drastically.

Or a Cautionary Tall Tale?

Obviously, there is a lesson in this for everyone, but first I should tell you that the incident with Shauna and her niece never happened. However, I can tell you it's not unlike the scenario I created for John when I met with him to discuss his personal risk management plan. I actually met John at a community event at about the time in his life described in the beginning of this story—before he became extremely wealthy from his IPO, and when he was considering purchasing the colonial. We were introduced through our wives who worked together on the community event. For that reason, we fell into a comfortable mode as we struck up a conversation.

He mentioned that he and his wife had fallen in love with a beautiful estate-like property upstate. He went on about his plans to build an equestrian center for his daughters, to house his friends in the guesthouse, to eventually build a vineyard, and, in time, to add a garage to house his antique motorcycle collection. I knew he wasn't bragging. I could tell he was genuinely passionate about his plans and he needed an ear to express them.

I congratulated him on his plans, and mentioned that I was a personal risk management specialist. I then asked him to give me a ballpark figure of what he thought his overall risk exposure would be. That opened the door to a conversation about his understanding, or lack thereof, of homeowners insurance, liability coverage, and, generally, the amount of exposure people in his position have. I shared that I work with a number of high-net-worth individuals who seem to do everything right when they get to the next level, but that most overlook their greater exposure to risks. He asked me what I do differently for these clients that he hasn't already done, so I told him.

I could see his brain working, and the newly formed sheen across his forehead told me he was growing uncomfortable with the conversation. Being the gentleman he is, he thanked me for my insight and then excused himself with a warm smile and a two-handed handshake. I thought that might be the last time I would see him. Two days later, my cell phone rang and an unknown number popped up. It was John, calling from his car phone to ask if I could visit with him and his wife at his home.

Now, four years and about $70 million of additional net worth later, John has a comprehensive risk management plan in place. It took a coordinated, collaborative effort with his advisory team, of which I am now a member. The plan includes an annual risk assessment, periodic appraisals, an annual update of his liability coverage, and a review of risk mitigation and security measures. There is even a response plan in place in the event of a kidnap/ransom situation.

Lessons Learned

I had always wondered what was going through John's mind during our first conversation when he became visibly uncomfortable over the topic of risk. So at an appropriate moment when we were alone, I asked him about it. "John, do you recall when we first met?" He replied that he sure did. I went on, "You really appeared to be upset when we were discussing your plans for your new home, and then I brought up your risk exposure. I really thought you were upset with me. What was going through your mind then?"

He paused and smiled. "It's not often someone tells me something about my personal finances that I don't already know. But that day I learned something I didn't know, and I realized at that moment that not knowing could have cost me dearly. Does that make sense?"

"Perfect sense" I replied.

Like all of my high net worth clients, John is extremely intelligent and financially astute. And, more so than most, he is also a planner. He takes care to set his sights and then follows his path with deliberate steps. But, when climbing the ladder of success and wealth, it's very easy to lose sight of the forest for the trees, especially if you are simply unaware of the dangers within. For John, and nearly every high net worth individual with whom I've worked, it wasn't immediately apparent that with more wealth comes greater exposure. What worked for them at the bottom of the ladder can't come close to providing the protection they need at the next level. As John learned before it was too late, nothing short of a comprehensive risk management plan is sufficient for protecting people of wealth from the unexpected.

WHAT RISKS ARE YOU FACING?

In the chapters that follow you will be introduced to a variety of risks facing high-profile and high net worth individuals. Consider this your risk management checklist as you evaluate your own situation. Chances are, there are several areas of exposure; but all you need is one to jeopardize all or part of what you've worked hard to build for you and your family.

In this digital age it is easier than ever to do many things on our own faster and more cost effectively than ever before. Experience reveals to me that along with this ease come costly errors, which most insurance consumers aren't even aware are happening. Listed here are the Top Five Insurance Planning Errors I come across as I meet with new clients.

THE TOP FIVE INSURANCE ERRORS PEOPLE MAKE PLANNING ON THEIR OWN

1. *Buying insurance like a commodity:* I hate to be the bearer of bad news to many of you self-doers out there, but insurance is not a commodity. The onslaught of advertising we hear on a daily basis from a variety of insurance companies leads us to believe that it is. After all, why not be able to negotiate, understand, and purchase a complex legal and financial instrument on your own by computer or 800 number in a matter of minutes and save a few dollars! Do you really understand all the forms, laws, and coverage nuances? Never mind the ability to be certain the coverage integrates as it should with other elements of your insurance portfolio. My experience reveals to me that better than 7 of 10 people get one or more critical pieces of the puzzle wrong when they decide they can be their own insurance professional.

2. *Insurance purchased from multiple agents/sources:* Clients with advanced insurance planning needs often have what I call a scattered insurance program when I first meet with them. They bought home, auto, umbrella, and valuables insurance from the agent that insures their primary residence. When they bought the vacation home on the lake, the local real estate agent referred the local agent and that person handles the vacation home. What comes next? Exactly—a boat for water-skiing and an old Jeep to drive around the mountains. The boat gets insured with one direct writing insurance company and the Jeep goes to another direct writer. Do we see a recipe coming together for what I call an insurance financial disaster?

3. *My insurance person is real nice:* Most insurance professionals *are* very nice, personable individuals. I consider it a prerequisite for the job as communication with and attention to my clients constitutes my entire day. Just because these folks are real nice does not make them great at their job. What do you perceive their job to be? I break the insurance community into two distinct groups. The first group I call Price Shoppers. You provide them with your basic information and they break from the starting gate and make their way around the insurance racetrack talking to the various players in the insurance market they believe will price

(continued)

your coverage the lowest. With some speed and a good whip-hand they hope to finish first with the cheapest price and win the order. The second group are the Risk Managers, true planners and fact finders. This group takes it slow and spends the time to learn about your lifestyle and goals, and has the tools to uncover all the exposures you face. After using their tools and knowledge they then embark on the design of a plan for you to transfer risk from your balance sheet to the insurance company. This plan then gets reviewed with you and your dream team to be sure all exposures are addressed and to provide risk-reducing strategies you can use going forward. The moral of the story here is to work with a professional at insurance planning and risk transfer. This will most likely be a nice person whose motivation includes pride in work and providing solutions to keep you out of trouble.

4. *Save a few dollars yet risk millions!:* All of us have heard it since we were children: Don't be penny-wise and pound-foolish! Give me a dollar for the number of conversations I've had with clients where they asked to strip away critical coverage so they could get to the number they have in mind for their insurance budget and I would be retired already. Insurance pricing can be a tricky lion to tame. Address this lion the wrong way and you may just lose your arm, if not more. The deductible provides the most effective pricing weapon you have at your disposal as a consumer. The question becomes one of risk and reward. I present the question to my clients this way: "Which check is easier for you to write, the one for the higher deductible of $10,000 on your home or the one for the $300,000 of dwelling coverage and $100,000 of valuables you are looking to remove?" The answer appears obvious; however, this illustrates where working with the right insurance professional can help you think of new ways to address risk and secure your financial future.

5. *Unaware of what to purchase:* Wouldn't it be great if you could go to a cardiologist's office without incurring the cost of paying the cardiologist and his technicians? Sure, just walk in, pay a reduced fee, take your time using the machinery, then evaluate the results yourself as they print out. With some luck it won't take as long as actually meeting with the cardiologist just to listen to him speak to you in medicalese. I don't know about you, but I would have no idea of what I am looking at and how to properly use

(continued)

THE TOP FIVE INSURANCE ERRORS PEOPLE MAKE PLANNING ON THEIR OWN (*Continued*)

that information going forward. How does this far-fetched idea relate to insurance? While your physical life is not at risk with insurance planning, your financial life could be. This relates to error #1. Personal insurance exposures come in several forms. These include the activities we participate in (boating, jet-skis, snowmobiles, ATVs, RVs, vacation homes, collectibles, public visibility, volunteering as board members, personal aviation, race driving, and more). Each of these opens a whole new set of insurance conversations and needs to be prescribed the right remedy to keep you out of harm's way. Don't limit your idea of personal planning to the products you hear advertised most. Analysis of your lifestyle, activities, and possessions is the surest way to see you are not leaving your wealth exposed.

CHAPTER 2

My-Oh-My, How Far You Have Come!

Please indulge me for a moment. I'd like you to take just 30 seconds to close your eyes, relax, and then think back to your first apartment. . . .

REMEMBER YOUR FIRST APARTMENT?

Did you see it? Did you take a look around? Remember the furniture, the posters on the wall, the shag carpet? I'm willing to bet that, when you opened your eyes, you had a smile on your face. It seems that the farther we have come from those earlier, simpler times, the more we can smile about them. And, oh, my, how far you have come.

Chances are your look back probably didn't end with a visit to your first apartment. If you're like most people, your mind probably took you on a quick journey through time—a fast-forward to your first home with your spouse; the home your kids grew up in, and finally, to the magnificent house you now call home. Whether that happened for you or not, the point I'm leading to is that you have come a long way. At each stop, your life grew richer (and not solely in monetary terms), but it also grew much more complicated. Sometimes, remembering whence we came can help place in a proper perspective not just what has changed, but also how those changes impact the way we navigate a more intricate lifestyle.

How Life at the Next Level Changes Everything

Consider your lifestyle when you bought your first home. You had just enough furniture to fill the rooms, and the only valuable things you had were the gifts from your wedding and your old LP collection. You may have had a couple of cars—one used, one new (probably leased). You worked for someone else, and you knew at any moment how much you had in the bank or your 401(k) within a hundred dollars. Your local agent took care of all of your protection needs: a standard homeowners policy with no endorsements, and insurance on your two cars bundled together with a 10 percent discount. No worries—life was great.

As you started earning more money, you probably moved into a larger house in a nicer neighborhood, with a larger garage to hold more toys. Your insurance agent was right on top of it, getting you more coverage and increasing your liability limits. He may have even recommended a personal property endorsement to cover the Rolex watch you splurged on because it was important to make a good impression on your clients.

With each move up the ladder, it was, essentially, rinse and repeat. Your agent was always there to make sure you had enough to cover your expanding lifestyle. It was all good because you knew he had your best interests at heart and would always take care of you. And then it happened.

It may have taken just a few years or maybe a couple of decades, but at some point you made it to the *next level*. You know, the level at which you can no longer count on both hands the different types of assets you hold; the level in which your net worth is tracked by a team of advisors; the level that puts you in the company of the most influential people in the state who need to go through your personal assistant in order to reach you. It's that point when, after you count it all up, you figure you could live comfortably for the rest of your life without working another day. But you still can't imagine that day ever coming. At the next level, you don't consider your lifestyle to be "rich" by any measure, just different from the way you were before you got there.

Okay, maybe that doesn't fit you exactly. But, no matter how or when you got there, chances are you arrived with your traditional view of risk protection intact. After all, what makes you think it should be any different? The same protections you've had all of these years have served you well, and your insurance agent has been with you each step of the way.

The problem is, just as you broke through to the next level, your agent probably hit his ceiling of competence. That doesn't make him a bad agent. He did everything you ever asked of him. But, just as you can't expect a general practitioner to perform open heart surgery on you (nor would you want him to), you can't expect an insurance generalist to be able to advise you on the intricacies of personal risk management for high net worth individuals—nor should you.

While you were busy climbing the ladder, the stakes involved, your exposures to risk, were growing exponentially. And, at some point, the traditional instruments of a property and casualty agent became dangerously insufficient. But you wouldn't have necessarily known that, and, in all likelihood, neither would your agent. If he did, he should have referred you to a risk management specialist the very moment your risks exceeded his capacity to protect you.

So, what exactly has changed in your life and your lifestyle that warrants a radically different approach to risk management? In the next five chapters we will help you count the ways. We begin in this chapter with, perhaps, your greatest risk exposure: your primary residence. It may not be your largest risk in dollar terms, but it can be your most complex, because there are so many facets and countless variables involved in protecting homes at the next level.

Your Primary Home Exposures at the Next Level

A successful entrepreneur was referred to me who had insured his home with a property and casualty agent for $2 million. He was concerned, as he should have been, that it wasn't nearly enough to replace his home should it suffer a total loss. But that was the maximum coverage available to him through this direct writer. Working through a carrier that specialized in high-end, rural properties, we determined that the actual replacement cost of his home was $3.3 million. Not only were we able to obtain the required coverage, we also added essential protections such as guaranteed rebuilding, replacement cost on contents, and a package of loss control services—none of which were readily available through his previous carrier.

A normal homeowners policy will usually suffice for normal homes in normal areas of coverage. But, if a higher-end home, made of custom materials and located in an outlying area, is damaged significantly, the costs to rebuild it are usually much higher due to the supply and demand for materials and experienced contractors and artisans. Carriers that specialize in the high-end property niche can provide broader coverage, and they will also assume the responsibility for establishing an accurate replacement value.

There are many other considerations when determining the risk management needs of high-end properties:

- If your home is more than 40 years old, there may be special insurance needs, such as an extra ordinance or law endorsement with extra high limits. It may also require guaranteed or extended replacement cost coverage available through specialized carriers.
- If your home has historic value, you will need to avoid functional replacement cost coverage and obtain a restoration cost homeowners policy with appropriate endorsements. Your coverage needs to be adequate

to cover the costs of contractors or architects that specialize in historic homes.

- If your home sits on a property that contains valuable landscaping and trees, you will need more expansive coverage for this added exposure.

Of course, this is merely a sampling of conditions that require expert assessments and a much more advanced approach to managing and controlling property risks.

Do I Really Need Flood Insurance?

Superstorm *Sandy* was a stark reminder that the most devastating part of a storm is usually the flooding that occurs as a result of storm surges. In the Midwest, overflowing rivers have wiped out small towns and farms. But, what most homeowners may not realize is that 25 percent of flood claims occur in areas that have low-to-moderate flood risk.[1]

Most homeowners are aware that their standard homeowners policies don't cover flood damage, so the decision not to obtain the extra coverage is usually a conscious one in which the homeowner weighs the risks. "It could never happen here," is typically as far as their risk assessment might go. While most homeowners may not live near a body of water, just about any home can be threatened by a heavy rain that could flood their basement because the surrounding soil couldn't absorb the overflow of water. In hilly areas, flooding from a heavy rain or flash flood can also cause the hill behind the house to collapse into a mudslide.

Now that we've dealt with the "it could never happen here" issue, let's explore the options luxury and custom homeowners should consider to fully insure their homes. As one would expect, super-storm *Sandy* unleashed a flood of calls into insurance agents and brokers looking into flood insurance. However, luxury homeowners soon learned that the coverage available in standard flood insurance policies is woefully inadequate. The maximum coverage available is $250,000 on structure and $100,000 on contents. The maximum coverage on valuables (artwork, collectibles, rare books, jewelry, furs) is $2,500 of its actual cash value. If your basement is finished with a game room, theater, family recreation room, the man cave, wine cellar you would be out of luck. The coverage for basements provided by standard flood insurance is limited to the equipment necessary to maintain basic living conditions such as furnaces, hot water heaters, washer/dryer, plumbing, electrical and some drywall.

The standard flood insurance policy is only intended to help homeowners get back on their feet and not to restore their home or possessions to their original condition. Of course, the exposure could leave luxury homeowners hundreds of thousands of dollars at risk, which is why specialized insurers offer both flood insurance coverage and excess flood insurance. The flood policy forms from specialized insurance companies, typically cover the basement, living expenses during rebuilding, and an overall higher dollar amount of coverage based on the replacement cost of the homes and belongings. Excess flood policies provide the increased coverage limits needed for the higher value homes. Homeowners with extensive valuables and collections should ensure they have the optimum coverage under separate valuables and collections policies.

The policies offering broader flood insurance coverage are available through blue-chip luxury carriers such as AIG, Firemen's Fund, ACE, and Chubb. Please see the chart in the appendix for additional details on the advantages of flood insurance from a specialized company.

Smart Homes, Radiant Heat, Home Theaters, Wine Cellars, Trophy Rooms, Indoor Pools, Gyms, Exotic Construction Materials, Climate Controls, Auto Showrooms, and Lots of Equipment to Keep It All Functioning

I'll never forget the nightmare one of my clients, Jared, experienced on just the third day he and his wife spent in their brand-new, 7,000-foot custom home. They had just finished a renovation that had cost them nearly $3 million. In addition to being an architectural beauty of a house, it was a technological wonder—a smart home with radiant heat, climate controls throughout, a home theater, a sophisticated security system, and an indoor waterfall, all of which could be controlled from anywhere in the world. And, of course, it was fashioned with the finest of aesthetic materials and appliances, many of which were imported from Italy.

They had just finished unloading their art collection so the interior designer could begin hanging paintings throughout the house, so they took some coffee out to the balcony to relax. Suddenly, Jared winced in reaction to an awful smell. He and his wife searched the house for the source, and then they saw it. It was like something out of bad horror film. A river of black, green, and brown mud-like goo was oozing under the door of their utility room, only this mud had a repulsive odor. As they looked outside they could see that the substance was pouring toward the side of their house and was oozing into their basement.

Looking up the hill, they realized what had happened. A sewer-line had ruptured near one of the homes at the top of the hill and was spewing sewage across a wide swath of properties beneath it. There was absolutely no way to stop it, and Jared could only watch as it enveloped his house.

Obviously, I wouldn't wish that experience on anyone, but this story does at least have a happy ending. I got the call while I was on ski trip. It took me several hours to get there. When I arrived the house was still being swallowed by the sewage. My clients were in shock, but out of the mass of people that had descended on their home, including emergency officials and county workers, they were the most relieved when they saw me. I had never seen anything like it, and I could only imagine what they were feeling after living in their new home for just three days. Ultimately, the house was condemned, and my clients spent a half-year in a hotel while their replacement home was being built.

The happy ending actually began more than two years ago when Jared showed me the blueprints for his dream home. That's when the appraisals began, scoping out the structural risks as well as the costs associated with many custom materials he had planned to use. The house was then appraised and risk assessments were conducted both during and after construction.

We insured their home with a policy that contained a guaranteed replacement cost provision, which, essentially, extends the amount of coverage to 100 percent of the dwelling limit on the policy. This was critical in order to account for the custom, one-of-a-kind features and unique materials used in the house that would surely increase in cost. That, coupled with an annual inflation adjustment, ensured my clients that they would be able to duplicate all of the high-end work to the greatest extent possible.

My clients knew they were building something very special and that it required much more than a typical homeowners policy to protect their masterpiece. I was fortunate to meet them through another client who had explained to them that such an exceptional property required exceptional protection. Unfortunately, nearly 70 percent of wealthy homeowners don't have the same message.

Equipment Breakdown Coverage

With manufacturer warranties and extended warranty coverage provided with some credit cards, most people might not see the need for equipment breakdown coverage. If an air conditioning system breaks down within the warranty period, it's replaced or repaired by the manufacturer *if it is caused by a defect*. But you and I both know that the point in time it will actually break down is one month *after* the expiration of the warranty period. Or, more commonly, the equipment breaks down due to damage that is not covered under warranty. What do you do then? A standard homeowners policy generally won't cover equipment breakdown, unless it is damaged in a storm or fire.

Equipment breakdown insurance will cover the cost to repair or replace home equipment any time it breaks down, with certain coverage restrictions of course. Considering all of the critical equipment contained in a large, custom home—heating and air conditioning systems, water heaters, ventilation, pool and hot-tub mechanics, backup generators, central vacuum systems, elevators, walk in freezers and so forth—something is bound to break at some point, and it usually happens at the most inopportune time. With standard warranties, you could wait days or weeks before it's repaired. With equipment breakdown insurance, repairs or replacements can happen within a matter of days.

Consider a family in the aftermath of a storm forced to use a generator to keep their power going. If the generator had broken down, it would have been impossible to run out and buy a new one. They would have been forced to go to a hotel, if they could find one with available rooms. With equipment breakdown insurance, their generator would have been replaced quickly, and any additional living expenses would have been covered.

At a cost of only $200 to $500 per year, equipment breakdown insurance is a relatively inexpensive coverage, especially for homes that are loaded with expensive and critical equipment.

Remodeling or Renovation Risks

When considering a remodel or renovation, many homeowners don't think about the need for additional coverage for damage or liabilities that occur during construction because they assume it is covered under their homeowners policy and/or the contractor's own insurance. That may not be the case, especially for large projects, which can multiply the risk of damage or injury to third parties. Generally, contractors are only responsible for a loss if they are found negligent, and homeowners policies may not be sufficient to address these additional exposures.

That's where Course of Construction (COC) coverage comes in. A COC policy covers losses due to damage, vandalism, theft of materials, and injuries to third parties. Other soft costs such as permits can also fall into the coverage provided by a COC policy. Generally, the amount of coverage is equal to the total project cost at completion. It is important to carefully review the contract with your contractor and identify who is responsible for providing COC coverage. Some contractors may refer to this as a Builders Risk policy. Be sure to ask your contractor to provide a certificate of insurance outlining the insurance coverage they have. You want to be sure if something goes wrong on the contractors part that there is an insurance company you can contact to step in and assist with a claim.

The Cottage for Mom   If I've heard it once, I've heard it at least a couple of dozen times from my clients: Their move to the country estates, 15 miles from town, would not have happened had the property not included a guesthouse for the in-laws. Many clients were just planning for periodic visits, but they also knew that, ultimately, the guesthouse would become their in-laws' permanent address. I say "in-laws" only because that's what they are for at least one side of the family. Also, in insurance parlance, a guesthouse or cottage is colloquially referred to as an "in-law apartment," because that's who usually winds up living in it.

Given the circumstances—a close family relative occupying a dwelling on the main property—one might think of it as a risk exposure that should be covered under a standard homeowners policy. But depending on the exact circumstances, that may not be the case. Any and all circumstances are subject to interpretation by any one insurance company. For the sake of brevity and a general understanding, we'll just consider the circumstance of a completely separate dwelling with its own entrance, utilities, and furnishings, which is supplied by the property hosts.

One insurance company, viewing this as a separate dwelling with the contents belonging to the owner of the main home, might only cover the contents up to $2,500. That would include the carpeting and appliances. It also might consider the personal property of the inhabitant as separate from that of the family in the main house, thus requiring a separate renters policy. In fact, it is always advisable for the inhabitant, be it a renter or an in-law, to have separate property coverage under a "renters" policy. Then again, if a family member is living there another company might view all contents as part of the main house, but would require an endorsement to cover the extra space and its contents.

The takeaway should be that insurance companies differ on how coverage is applied in an in-law apartment situation, and each situation must be considered for its specific risk exposure, which will ultimately dictate the type and amount of coverage. When the cottage renter is not family that person is responsible for purchasing their own renters policy to cover their personal property and liability.

The City Apartment   City living is very exciting! The restaurants, nightlife, theater, museums, skyscrapers and constant hum of activity are all at your doorstep. Couple that with the amenities of living in a luxury coop or condominium building and some would say you are living the dream. That dream does have some perils that I often see many coop and condominium apartment owners overlook as they believe the coop or condo association is responsible for everything. Coop or condo associations have limited responsibility and it is important to understand what you are responsible for.

Two documents provided by the association can act as your guide to understanding the coverage you need. One is the by-laws of the association. The second is generally known as a statement of Covenants, Conditions, and Restrictions (or CC&R's). Duties in the event of loss, the portion of the building that you are responsible for and insurance the association has for itself are provided in these documents.

Coop/condo policies are designed to cover what the association does not. This includes your personal property, personal liability for your family, reimbursement for loss of use of the apartment, some structural items including renovations you do, amounts you be assessed by the association in the event of a loss and limited coverage for valuables. Often I hear clients say my building is new what can go wrong. Recently I received a call from a client whose floors warped due to water damage from an apartment above his. Another client renovated his bathroom in his penthouse apartment and the new pipe burst while he was out causing water damage he is liable for to several apartments below his.

The cost of coop/condo insurance usually is very reasonable, especially for the newer, more secure buildings that also have 24 hour doormen. The specialized insurance companies provide an appraisal service to determine the amounts of coverage to repair structural items, your personal property and note items of higher value.

Who's Watching the Help?   It happens innocently enough. A Wall Street executive comes home after an evening of drinks and greets his housekeeper with a sly smile and a risqué remark about her "maid's uniform." As she usually does, she dismisses it as harmless fun. However, the next time could be different. If she ever felt the need to "get her fair share," she could easily set him up by hiding a hidden camera with a full view. It would be a clear case of sexual harassment costing tens or even hundreds of thousands of dollars.

The tabloids are rife with stories of nannies and house staff turning on their employers. Actress Sharon Stone's nanny of four years accused her with charges of racial harassment, sweatshop conditions, and wrongful termination. Then there was California gubernatorial candidate Meg Whitman's undocumented housekeeper, who turned against her and created a high-profile scandal that essentially cost her the election.

My files contain numerous instances of claims by personal employees, some of which may have been legitimate, but many of which were probably frivolous. One client fired a gardener for constantly being late to work. The gardener sued my client for wrongful termination, claiming that work hours were never established. Another client fired a housekeeper for poor performance. She then sued for discrimination and wrongful termination after my client replaced her with a younger and more attractive housekeeper.

Fortunately, my clients had the proper type of coverage and risk management controls in place.

If the Wall Street executive, or Stone, or Whitman had purchased "nanny coverage," otherwise known as Employment Practices Liability Coverage (EPLI), they may have been protected against claims by household staff for wrongful termination, sexual harassment, and discrimination.

Wealthy families with personal employees have tremendous risk exposures at many levels, and many either underestimate the risk or fail to put the proper controls in place. Chapter 4 goes into more depth on the risk management techniques wealthy families need to undertake when managing household staff.

Time to Host the Annual Gala Benefit Ball   My clients, David and Janelle, recently called me with the news that they would be hosting this year's annual gala benefit ball for their charity organization. Janelle couldn't hide her joy at the chance to showcase her home, but David sounded especially stressed, and with good reason. Even before he became a client, he and I had discussions about the special risks associated with these types of events. Their magnificent home, with beautiful gardens and expansive grounds, was the site of their daughter's wedding which was attended by 300 people, including my wife and me. We knew them and their daughter through our association with the charity.

Although David wasn't yet my client, I did find an opportune moment before the wedding to raise the issue of special event liabilities. At the time, he was extremely preoccupied with his business, which had been experiencing some heavy headwinds from new SEC regulations. He had turned all matters concerning the wedding over to his wife. When I mentioned that he should consider the risk exposure of a home-hosted wedding, and that it was not likely to be adequately covered by his homeowners and umbrella policies, he thanked me and said he would have Janelle look into it. The next time I spoke with either of them was at the wedding.

Shortly after their daughter's wedding, David and Janelle attended another wedding at the home of one of David's business associates. It was a similar setting—a courtyard wedding that seated about the same number of guests. The family went all-out, engaging the finest restaurant in town to cater the affair, hiring a well-known local jazz group for entertainment, and stocking the outdoor bar with the finest liquors and wines. They even rented a couple of 15-passenger vans to shuttle guests to and from the nearby hotels. This wedding had all of the earmarks of a truly special event.

Then tragedy struck. The hosts were careful to arrange for designated drivers for anyone who didn't take a ride back to town in their passenger vans. But, with nearly 300 guests, it's virtually impossible to account for every intoxicated person. One, the maid of honor's boyfriend, Jason, stormed out of the reception following a heated argument with the groom. Several people went out to chase him down, but he vanished in the fog that had enveloped the property. The last thing anyone heard was screeching tires and the winding sound of the young man's Porsche.

Later, the court would hold that, although the hosts were not liable for Jason's death, they were part liable for the critical injuries of the three people in the car he hit when he ran a red light at a fog-shrouded intersection. Jason's blood alcohol content was just over the legal limit. The court awarded the claimants $10 million for future medical claims and pain and suffering. David has suffered many sleepless nights since that verdict.

David and Janelle called to ask me to work with them on putting together a risk management strategy for another gala event. They understood that it would require a complete assessment of their risk exposure as it applied to the event and, ultimately, that any specific strategy would have to be coordinated with their existing risk management plan.

The assessment covered all possible risks, including bodily injury and property liability, and host liquor liability, all the way down to the theft or damage of the sterling silverware, which has limited coverage in homeowners policies. We even discussed taking out an event cancellation policy. David and Janelle were surprised to learn that most of our work involved risk reduction and control techniques that would actually reduce their insurance costs.

Thankfully, the event went off without a hitch, and the gracious hosts became overnight society celebs. They have since worked with my firm to implement a complete risk management plan.

Who Owns This House, Anyway?   Many of my clients live in homes they don't technically own. No, they're not renters, and they certainly aren't squatters. Wealthy homeowners commonly place their home in a trust to facilitate its transfer to family members at a later date. The most common practice is the establishment of a Qualified Personal Residence Trust (QPERT), which gives the property rights to your heirs immediately after you die. The arrangement allows you to remain in the home for a specific number of years. This has become an especially popular method of transferring property during times of depressed home prices, because the current value is locked in, and it is ultimately taxed at the gift tax rate, which includes a $1 million exemption.[2]

Residences held in a trust can create some unique loss exposures that require a special insurance arrangement. Depending on the insurance company, the named insured on the policy should be the trust, and the beneficiary or founder of the trust (typically the occupant) should be listed as an additional named insured. This provides protection for the interest everyone has in the structure and the contents of the property.

This applies to the many other forms of ownership, such as family partnerships, LLCs, corporations, and Life Estate/Life Tenancy, which are designed to ultimately transfer the property to heirs or other parties. The important element of all these arrangements is to have all parties listed on the policy as a named insured so each has his or her interest protected.

Your Vacation Home(s)—Where You Like to Relax and Play with Those Cool Toys   When you bought your first vacation home, you probably insured it as you normally would, accepting the fact that your premium would be about 20 percent higher than a primary homeowners policy. If you rented it out during parts of the year, you grudgingly went along with the extra 20 percent premium landlords must pay. And, hopefully, you knew about the need for increased liability insurance via an umbrella policy. Essentially, with some additional coverage to protect your boat, snowmobiles, and other toys, you were done.

But, at the next level, bigger and multiple vacation homes can create bigger and multiple liabilities. One of my clients, a retired attorney, has a vacation property in upstate New York consisting of a farmhouse, a barn and 160 acres of land. The property is prime for deer hunting, target shooting, and riding his Jeeps and ATVs off-road. When his family is not using it, his friends and relatives converge on the property for long weekends to take up those activities with full use of his house and vehicles. And, when the property is vacant, third-party hunters roam his land hunting for deer. Needless to say, his potential legal liabilities are large and numerous.

It was suggested that he take measures to mitigate his risk by limiting the use of his home, and making his property less accessible to third-party hunters. He had no problem with putting up additional fencing and signs to deter the hunters, but his generosity wouldn't allow him to limit the use of his home by friends. So, in addition to expanding his personal umbrella liability policy, he attached some fairly strict rules to its usage.

It's also not unusual for wealthy families to own multiple vacation properties. These are strewn throughout the country, as much for their enjoyment as for diversifying their real estate portfolio. Then they discover that insuring each property requires navigating the special conditions of each state while dealing with the underwriting nuances of multiple insurance companies. An incremental, uncoordinated approach to insuring multiple properties usually results in an unruly web of expensive policies beset with complicated conditions and special deductions that may not provide the desired quality of coverage and service.

We have found many families in this situation. One in particular owned five homes in four states, with a total replacement cost of $15 million. Like most property owners, they purchased their insurance policies on demand, each with enough coverage to cover the replacement cost of a particular property. In addition to the high cost of insuring five properties this way, they expended a considerable amount of time and energy just to deal with the individual preferences of the local insurers.

Applying a more sophisticated strategy, we recommended a solution that takes advantage of the *geographic spread of risk*. This treats the five homes as a group. Insuring all five homes as if the whole group might be destroyed all at once is not only inefficient, it is statistically impossible. Using a blanket policy approach, I can determine the maximum loss that could occur from any one event, and then apply that amount to the blanket policy coverage limit. So, rather than insuring five homes for $15 million, the family might only need $12 million.

These policies can be highly customized around the family's ability to accept high levels of risk with unique deductibles that can result in significant savings. In this case, the family was able to save nearly 50 percent in premium costs. But, because blanket policies are customizable and each is unique, they do require a significant amount of due diligence using the sophisticated techniques of a qualified risk management specialist.

Just the Tip of the Iceberg   As I previously indicated, when it comes to fully protecting the homes of wealthy clients, there are many facets and countless variables that must be considered. The risk exposures discussed in this chapter only scratch the surface of what high net worth homeowners face. In the coming chapters, I will go into greater depth with other common homeowner risks, such as household staff employment, maintaining valuables and collectibles, and how far your homeowners liability protection will follow you as trot across the globe.

The overriding takeaway here is that nothing short of a thorough onsite assessment of all of these risks, along with continuous property appraisals, will provide the essential risk management solutions the high net worth homeowner needs at the next level.

CHAPTER 3

Life Is Too Short to Drink Cheap Wine

A friend of a client of mine, a somewhat eccentric but highly successful real estate mogul, was a connoisseur of fine wines and expensive cigars. Geoffrey was also a self-proclaimed wise-guy who gained immense satisfaction by profiting from loopholes in contracts and the law. On one of his many trips to Europe, he purchased a box of 45 "Behike" cigars made by Altadis of Spain. Named for the tribal chief of the ancient Taino tribe from Cuba, only 4,000 of the limited Cohiba brand cigars were released. At $19,000 per box, each time he lit up he burned $420.

As he did with all of his valuables and collectibles, Geoffrey had the box of cigars insured to protect them against hazards, such as fire. After he smoked all 45 cigars, he filed an insurance claim stating that the cigars had been "consumed by a series of small fires." Of course, the insurance company took him to court, but they were stunned when the judge found in favor of Geoffrey with an order to pay the full claim. The court found no specific language in the policy excluding any particular kind of fire—the exact loophole Geoffrey was counting on. Triumphant once again, he swaggered into his bank with the check. The moment he received his deposit slip, he was arrested and charged with 45 counts of arson—one for each cigar. Having run out of loopholes, he served two years in a state prison.

You probably figured out that this didn't actually happen. It's an urban legend going way back, and it was even made into a song by Brad Paisley. Anyone with a rudimentary knowledge of insurance and the law could have debunked the story. We know, for instance, that insurance policies usually state that claims cannot be paid when the loss is caused by the deliberate actions of the policyholders. We also know that you can't be charged with arson for destroying your own property, as long as there is no intent to commit fraud. Finally, if the court ordered the claim to be paid, then there was no fraud, which means there was no arson. But that's neither here nor there, because it didn't happen.

So, why did I go down this path? Aside from its being a mildly entertaining story, it illustrates three important elements of this chapter. First, wealthy people do like to enjoy the finer things in life, whether it's sharing a fine bottle of wine, or being surrounded by a collection of museum-quality fine art. For many people collecting valuables is a passion, but it also has become the alternative of choice for investors who seek diversification beyond the stock market.

Second, there is virtually nothing that can't be insured. If it has value and can be appraised, there is a specialty insurance policy that will cover it; yet, remarkably, as many as 60 percent of collectors don't have insurance coverage for their valuables. It's estimated that more than 80 percent of wealthy collectors are underinsured.

Finally, most people aren't quite as conversant in the language of insurance as our friend Geoffrey. In fact, for many of the 60 percent mentioned earlier, it's not until after they have learned the hard way of the huge chasm that exists between the protections provided in standard homeowners policies and specialty insurance policies. Many high net worth people are still being serviced by their property-casualty agents who, although they are mostly well-intentioned, either don't have the capacity to educate their clients on their heightened risk exposures, or don't have a relationship with expert appraisers.

For the 30 or 40 percent of collectors who do understand their exposure, and who may have purchased specialty insurance, many make the big mistake of failing to actively manage their collection. In certain collection niches, values have increased markedly. For instance, jewelry collectors who had their items appraised for insurance five years ago would receive about half their current value today due to gold and silver's meteoric rise. The same is true for fine artwork, which has become a favored asset class by investors and collectors alike.

What many collectors are learning, often the hard way, is that there is much more to collecting valuables than shelling out the money for them. Even those who have taken the initial steps of buying the right kind of coverage are finding that, without a deliberate strategy for actively managing their valuables and collectibles, they may have a serious and expensive gap in coverage.

This chapter details the risk exposure of owning valuables and collectibles, and it outlines the steps to take to ensure your protection doesn't come up short should disaster strike.

A LOOK AT MANAGING VALUABLES AND COLLECTIBLES SCHEDULES

Walking through the homes of clients who are passionate art collectors can be the equivalent of taking a stroll through a museum. Keeping the collection safe and properly valued does require some planning, which these collectors are happy to do in order to preserve the valuable works they have acquired.

The Collection

Anyone who owns fine artwork has to realize that the possibility of damage exists even when you have taken steps to prevent it. I've seen instances where rare masterpieces were damaged in ways their owners could not have anticipated. In one case, a Renoir took the brunt of a large flower vase that was accidently dropped from a second floor balcony. The vase (which was also a high-value collectible) crashed to the floor, splashing water over the painting.

Perhaps the most notable case of the "unimaginable" occurred with a Picasso owned by casino developer Steve Winn at a party he hosted in 2006. The painting, which he had recently sold for $139 million, was still on display in the gallery where the party took place. In front of a stunned crowd, he inexplicably jammed his elbow through the painting. Experts were able to restore the painting, but the sale was canceled because its value was cut by a third.

Insurance is the primary instrument we use to transfer a risk we could not otherwise undertake financially to someone who can. But managing the risk of damage or theft of fine artwork doesn't end with an insurance policy. It requires a continuous process of proactive management to ensure that the value of the collection doesn't outpace the coverage.

Importance of Actively Managing the Art Schedule

Before fully immersing themselves in the high-stakes world of fine art collecting, most collectors begin by sticking their toe in the water. They purchase two or three pieces here or there, and then periodically add to their collection. For fledgling collectors, the essential task of documenting, valuing, tracking, and insuring a small collection is one they might enjoy doing themselves, especially as they seek to learn more about their new passion. But, as their passion grows, along with their collection, these tasks can be daunting, which increases the risk of improper valuation. This is especially true for active collectors who are constantly buying, selling, or loaning their works. At some point, nothing short of a dedicated system for managing the art schedule will suffice for ensuring the optimum level of coverage for their collection. The same collection management system can also be very useful in tax and estate planning.

The challenge for art collectors is that, unlike other market-based assets such as stocks, bonds, and even real estate, there is no active market with a steady number of buyers and sellers bidding on prices. So, valuation is more of an art than a science based on a number of variables. As such, the value of art, both individually and collectively, is in a constant state of flux.

Depending on the global art market for any particular genre or artist, a piece valued at $1 million today could be worth five times that amount in a few short years. Without the capacity to track and document the changing values, the coverage could come up very short in the event a piece is damaged. I strongly recommend that high-value artwork be appraised by an expert once every three or four years, at a minimum.

Artwork is unique in that its value is tied to its provenance, that is, to its historical record, if it has one. Knowing the history of a piece and its lineage in terms of owners is important, especially if it is the work of a famous artist or one who is deceased. It also minimizes any concerns over its authenticity. Without proper documentation, the integrity of a piece's provenance could come into question, which could drastically lower its value.

If the artwork is purchased from a gallery, dealer, or at an auction, the seller is responsible for providing the buyer with the provenance, along with a certificate of authenticity. If the work is from a new but promising artist, there won't be much in the way of provenance documentation; however, the certificate of authenticity will be extremely important, especially if there is a possibility of reselling it in the future.

Owning any collection of valuables entails myriad complex risks and financial exposures requiring specific expertise in their assessment, management, and mitigation. High-value artwork can be especially complex because no two pieces are exactly the same; certainly no two collections are the same. There are simply no off-the-shelf risk management solutions for serious art collectors. The ideal time to implement a comprehensive risk management plan is when the collection is still small. However, with the stakes so high, it's never too late, either.

At a minimum, high-value art collectors should follow these essential steps to ensure they have the optimum protections:

- *Put the best risk management team together, including an independent insurance advisor who specializes in risk management.* He or she should have access to specialty insurance carriers, appraisers, and loss prevention advisors.
- *Utilize a reliable system for tracking, documenting, and valuing the collection on a scheduled basis.* Specialized collection management software programs are available, or it can be outsourced to a risk management specialist. In either case, records and documentation should be stored offsite in a secure location.

- *Consult with a risk mitigation specialist.* Security technology is advancing at digital speed. Risk mitigation specialists always have a finger on the pulse of the latest and most effective systems. They can also advise on fire and smoke detection systems, display locations, and storage and evacuation plans.
- *Maintain the proper insurance coverage.* The best risk management plan in the world cannot mitigate away all risks, which is why it's important to transfer that risk to an insurance company that specializes in high-end collectibles. More important, find an insurance advisor or broker who specializes in risk management for high net worth individuals. Their expertise in the area of risk management can be invaluable.

Insuring the Title of Your Artwork

Whoever said that "possession is nine-tenths of the law" probably knew very little about the art world. And, if fine art owners are complacent about that old common-law precept, they could be in for a rude awakening should their artwork's title of ownership ever be questioned. In fact, the greatest risk in owning fine art is not damage or theft; it is the risk of a *defective legal title*. This is the risk that a work of art legally belongs to someone else, even though it was purchased legitimately. If that sounds like a nightmare scenario for an art owner, it is.

The biggest mistake art collectors can make is to dismiss the risk of defective title, in the belief that they had purchased their works legitimately with legal title. There is a dangerous misconception that the risk is small because it is relatively small compared with real estate purchases. The problem is that a real estate title is a completely different animal than a legal title with artwork. The database for real estate titles is vast, digitally accurate, and managed by each of the 50 states. It is far easier to uncover title defects in a real estate transaction than it is to fully ascertain the ownership lineage of a work of art. At one time, sales of fine art were kept confidential, so there may be gaps in the ownership records.

Although galleries and art dealers are obligated to guarantee the legal title of their artwork for a number of years, the ensuing legal tussle almost guarantees that the purchaser will walk away empty-handed. Galleries and art dealers are generally just intermediaries between a seller and a buyer, so they rely heavily on representations made by the actual seller regarding the legal title.

So, if a title problem arises, the intermediary will typically pursue the seller for recourse, leaving the buyer, who has little if any recourse against the seller, in a state of limbo. If the seller is deceased, bankrupt, or out of the country, the intermediary will have great difficulty in pursuing a judgment.

If the artwork was purchased through an auction house, there will probably be a provision in the contract that allows it to rescind a sale at any time in the event of a title claim.

Even if the purchaser is able to learn the identity of the current owner, there is a likelihood that prior ownership can't be accurately traced to the original owner. This makes the management of legal risks virtually impossible.

The next biggest mistake art collectors make is assuming that their homeowners policy covers their legal title risks. While it's true that some property insurance carriers offer endorsements that will cover some of the costs of defending legal title, they often will fall way short of what the art owner will shell out in legal costs. In addition, these floaters tend to place most of the burden of proving a valid claim on the art owner. For instance, if the insurance carrier determines that the owner could have or should have found out about the title defect at the time of purchase, the claim could be denied. The bottom line with homeowners policy endorsements is that they are flimsy at best, and they won't provide the level of protection for high-end works of art.

That leaves us with the one solution that can provide protection against legal title risks—that is, art title insurance provided by a licensed art title insurance company. It is the only form of coverage that can provide art owners with a full defense of title, as well as a financial guarantee of the value of the work. And this coverage extends to a lifetime of ownership by the insured, heirs, or any trust or tax-based entity to which the art work is transferred. Following a simple application process that includes documentation of the purchaser's own knowledge about the works, as well as the provenance and exhibit history, a onetime premium payment will immediately cover an individual work or a collection in four general risk categories without exclusions:

1. Contemporary and historical theft
2. Import and export defects
3. Liens and encumbrances
4. Illegal or unauthorized sales

Legal title risk is not limited to art collectors. Collectors of rare books, manuscripts, rare instruments, estate jewelry, and vintage automobiles face the same risk with tremendous financial exposure. Even well-intended sellers who guarantee the accuracy of ownership lineage can't be 100 percent certain of their facts. So, if there is one particular risk that should keep art owners up at night, it is the legal title risk, at least until they take the essential risk management measure of obtaining legal title insurance.

Where Is Your Artwork Showing This Month?

Many art collectors are only too pleased to show their finest pieces at galleries and museums. The pride they feel is not unlike that of parents when their child is showcased in a play or sporting event. From a practical or financial standpoint, it can also help to enhance the market value of the pieces as well as the collector's reputation in the art world. On the downside, art owners open themselves up to a number of risks beyond what their insurance might cover.

Take, for example, the high-profile case involving the Philadelphia Museum of Art in 2010. The museum had consigned two paintings, worth $1.5 million, to a gallery in 2006. Unbeknownst to the museum, the gallery's owner sold the paintings and kept the proceeds. The gallery owner was convicted of 29 counts of grand larceny and one count of scheming to defraud.

The museum, which had a $100 million "all risk" insurance policy, filed a claim with its insurer, who argued that it was the museum's negligence that was responsible for the loss. The insurer said that the museum should have been more diligent in its background check and oversight of the gallery. The insurer also found an exclusion for the "all risk" coverage—in this case, theft by deception—which they said rendered the claim invalid. The case is still being litigated in the courts, and, of course, the museum has yet to recover its losses.

This is a cautionary tale for any art owner who wants to ensure maximum protection for valuable artwork under any circumstance. Loaning or consigning art to a gallery or an art show requires that art owners not only understand their own coverage, but also the coverage the recipient has on its own. It can get especially complicated if the recipient is out of state where the level of coverage may differ. For instance, if you live in Arizona, you don't have to be concerned with hurricanes. But if the artwork is loaned to a museum in Miami, it would be important to know the specific coverage it has to protect it against natural disasters.

Before loaning or consigning artwork, art owners should have their own policies as well as that of the recipient thoroughly reviewed by their attorney and/or a personal risk management advisor. And, as always, their schedules should be updated with the most current valuations.

Jewelry—I Lost My Bracelet in Barcelona

Nothing has captured the attention of the investment world over the last decade more than the meteoric rise in gold and silver prices. From 2001 to 2012, gold has appreciated by more than 500 percent, and silver prices have increased nearly 600 percent. And many see the prospect of significant upside from there. Of course, as go precious metal prices, so goes the price of jewelry.

TEN QUESTIONS ABOUT YOUR ART COLLECTION AT HOME

Here are 10 questions to carefully consider in assessing how much exposure there is with your art collection:

1. Is the home where the art is located your primary or secondary home or both?
2. Is there a staff to manage the home?
3. Does the home or property play host to events?
4. Where are the highest-value pieces displayed or stored?
5. Is the home alarmed and is the alarm activated?
6. Do you have a disaster plan in place that includes the art?
7. Does the home have environmental controls in place regarding temperature and humidity?
8. Is there an inventory or proper documentation? Where are those records kept?
9. Are there lawn sculptures/installations on the premises?
10. Does the location of the home increase its exposure to natural disaster?

Except for those people, caught in the carnage of the economic downturn, who turned their gold and silver jewelry in for cash, the sharp spike in precious metal prices may have escaped the attention of many owners of fine jewelry. Recently, a client had her fine jewelry collection appraised for the first time in six years. She was absolutely astonished to learn her collection, which was valued at about $360,000 in 2006, appraised for more than $680,000 in 2012. Even those who had their collections valued in the last three years were surprised to find out they had appreciated by as much as 50 percent.

While that is certainly good news for those who found their way to an appraiser and updated their insurance coverage, where does that leave most of the other jewelry collectors who, on average, are underinsured by as much as 80 percent?[3] Worse, where does it leave the estimated 60 percent of fine jewelry owners who think their homeowners insurance policy is sufficient to protect their valuables? "Severely exposed" is the only thing that comes to mind.

TEN QUESTIONS TO ASK YOUR ART STORAGE FACILITY

1. What is the exact location of the facility?
2. Does the facility have a disaster preparedness plan?
3. What is the expertise and the background of the staff?
4. Does the facility utilize an inventory management system?
5. What are the environmental conditions within the facility?
6. What level of fire and security protection is present at the facility?
7. How and where will the collection be stored within the facility?
8. What is the construction of the building?
9. Does the facility also provide packing and shipping services?
10. Is the facility an approved TSA-certified cargo-screening facility?

High-End Jewelry Requires High-End Appraisals

We've already touched on the importance of more frequent appraisals in light of booming precious metals prices. Although diamonds haven't see the kind of appreciation as gold and silver, high-grade, large-karat diamonds—the kind favored by wealthy jewelry collectors—have seen annual returns of 4 to 7 percent over the last decade.[4] But, a true jewelry aficionado or investor will also latch on to some of the more precious gem stones, such as rubies, sapphires, and tanzanites, which can fetch even higher prices. The market for authentically rare gems has nothing but upside and is subject to price spikes, which should be monitored for appraisal purposes.

While high-quality gold and silver jewelry can mostly match the price appreciation of the underlying metals, high-quality vintage jewelry can sometimes outpace it. The pricing of vintage jewelry is driven not only by the price of metals, but also by its provenance, especially if it originates from one of the great jewelry masters, such as Cartier, Chaumet, or Fabergé. Vintage jewelry pieces are valued as much for their unique craftsmanship as they are for their metal or gem content. Appraising exceptional pieces of jewelry for authenticity and uniqueness requires exceptional expertise and certainly should not be left to your run-of-the-mill jewelry appraiser.

Homeowners Policies Just Don't Cut It

It's a mystery to me why so many owners of high-end jewelry or other valuables still rely on their homeowners personal property coverage. They must know that personal property coverage is limited to $2,500 to $5,000 per item as well as a maximum amount for any one claim. Or, perhaps they know that, but they have completely lost track of the value of their items. To the credit of some jewelry owners, they have at least "scheduled" the items by adding a separate floater or endorsement on their homeowners. While this can provide better protection, high-end jewelry owners could still be greatly disappointed.

A future client of mine took a trip to Barcelona, Spain, and as she is accustomed to doing, she travels adorned, neck to wrists, with very expensive jewelry. On any given day, she could be wearing as much as $100,000 worth of jewelry. While rushing to catch a taxi, the clasp on her $10,000 diamond-and-ruby bracelet came loose, and as she was climbing into the cab, it fell to the ground. She was too frantic to notice.

When she contacted her property and casualty agent, she was shocked to learn that her homeowners would not cover the loss. Of course, she never bothered to read the policy, and her agent never bothered to educate her on the limitations. Even if her jewelry were covered for loss, the coverage only provides for actual cash value reimbursement, not replacement value, which could be substantially higher—another lesson learned the hard way.

Like art collections, jewelry collections typically start out small and grow gradually until they can become unmanageable from a documentation and scheduling standpoint. Or, a collection is inherited by heirs who haven't the foggiest idea of how to insure it. For all of the same reasons mentioned in the prior section on artwork, an extensive jewelry collection requires a proactive management system for tracking, documenting, and appraising. At a minimum, jewelry collectors should take the following steps to ensure optimum coverage for their collection:

Inventory, Inventory, and then, Inventory Again   A current and well-documented inventory is vital, especially when a loss occurs. But it is equally critical if the collection is to be transferred to a new location, or if it has been more than a few years since it has been appraised. All items should be photographed or videotaped as they are added to the collection, then uploaded to a secure data storage site.

Use Independent, Expert Appraisers   Most valuable articles schedules only require an estimate of current values for items under $2,500. While a sales receipt and a general description may suffice for lower-valued items, it is not likely to be adequate for assessing market value or actual replacement cost. If it can be left open to interpretation by the insurer, it almost never benefits the owner. Issues of provenance, diamond cut, gold quality, vintage, and purchase location are all critical in determining the replacement value, yet can be broadly interpreted without documentation only an expert appraiser can provide.

Get the Right Kind of Coverage   If you haven't yet noticed, I have a particular bias against using standard homeowners insurance to protect against the risks of a wealthy lifestyle, primarily for the reason that it just doesn't cut it. And, there's no clearer case for upgrading your scheduled coverage than with the limitations on jewelry and valuables protections. At a minimum, your valuables insurance coverage should include the following:

- *Market value coverage:* Designed to act as a buffer against price spikes and appreciation over time, this provision will pay up to 150 percent of the scheduled amount to cover actual replacement cost. It's important to update your schedules to ensure this benefit keeps pace with increasing market values.
- *Blanket coverage:* This type of coverage is essential if you have a large collection that includes a lot of lower-value items that don't require scheduling. While each may not be of high value individually, collectively they can add up to a significant number. Specialty insurance companies provide the ability to cover groups of items that establishes overall coverage.
- *Loss prevention:* Working with a specialty carrier you can receive specialized services to prevent loss, including expert consultations on security systems. It will also provide screening services for hiring household staff. Some will even provide assistance in the evacuation of valuables ahead of natural disasters.

Other essential features of valuables coverage include:

- Diminution of market value
- Worldwide coverage
- Pair and set clause
- Breakage and damage
- Zero deductible
- Choice of repair and replacement vendor
- Cash payment option

To Vault or Not to Vault   Most policies will reduce your premium if you store your valuables in a bank vault. This typically requires a special scheduling of items to be vaulted that includes a timetable of their use. This often requires separate premium pricing when items are removed from the vault frequently or for a length of time. Of course, some coverage may not extend to the loss of items due to a bank robbery or the destruction of the bank, so there is an element of risk. Some insurers will recommend an in-home vault built to certain specifications. The decision whether to use a bank vault or a home vault will typically come down to individual circumstances, preferences, type and extent of collection, and any coverage exclusions.

NOW TO THE WINE CELLAR FOR A VERTICAL TASTING OF LAFITE

Wine lovers tend to be among the most passionate of collectors. Because the fine wine market is so vast, transparent, and relatively affordable compared with other collectibles, it's not uncommon to see a wine collection grow quickly, from a storage unit located in the pantry to a full-scale, temperature-controlled wine cellar with its own generator. Through frequent acquisitions and escalating market values, a $5,000 collection can grow to $50,000 fairly quickly.

Wine lovers, lost in their enthusiasm, tend to overlook their financial exposure or underestimate the value of their collection, which is why more than half are considered to be drastically underinsured. Yet, there aren't many types of collectibles more fragile and more susceptible to disaster than a collection of wine bottles. All it takes is your prize bottle of Château Pétrus 1982 to slip from your hands to turn it into a $62,000 puddle of red liquid and broken glass. So, are you covered?

Speaking of which, it's always kind of fun to recount some stories of fateful moments in wine, especially when the endings are not completely sad. The one that stands out for many wine enthusiasts is the time when William Sokolin, a renowned and very wealthy wine merchant, brought his bottle of 1787 Chateau Margaux to a dinner soirée. This was in 1989, so he certainly wasn't bringing it to drink as it had long been reduced to vinegar. Rather he brought it in attempt to sell it for his $500,000 asking price.

Bottles of that vintage don't usually sell for that price, mainly because they're undrinkable. But, they may have historic value as did this one, which included the initials *TJ* for Thomas Jefferson, a substantial wine collector in his own right. With no takers, he grabbed his bottle to leave, and as he turned to bid the other guests adieu, a waiter bumped his arm, freeing the bottle to fall to its demise.

The not-too-sad ending is that Sokolin did have his bottle insured for $225,000, its more appropriate market value, so he was happy to take his cash consolation prize and go on collecting valuable wines.

In addition to the typical risks associated with collectibles, such as theft and breakage, wine is susceptible to a far more insidious risk—spoiling or deterioration—which is not an insurable risk. Nothing so shocks a wine enthusiast as the sour, gaseous odor of vinegar that whiffs up his nose as he pulls the cork from a $500 bottle of wine in front of discriminating guests. Any number of factors can contribute to spoiling—extreme temperatures, dampness or dryness, or even organic causes. In fact, outside of housing a wine collection in an earthquake zone, the risk of spoilage or deterioration is considered to be far greater than breakage or theft.

Valuing the Wine Cellar

Valuing wines, especially the rarified variety, is a specialty that shouldn't be left to amateurs. Many lower-valued wines can be appraised by simply researching their prices using one of the many wine pricing calculators available online. Older bottles or varieties that can exceed $1,000 should be independently appraised, in part so they can be individually scheduled on your wine insurance policy, but also because the market value for high-end wines can be influenced by factors other than supply and demand.

Wines with historical value need to be assessed for their provenance, not to mention the possibility of fraud. The prices of wines of great value and limited quantities can be influenced by more subjective factors, such as the preferences and competitiveness of the most avid collectors. With high-value wine becoming more of a global market, it's more difficult to determine the market value when Russian collectors are competing with Chinese collectors for the same wine. In the end, it comes down to what someone is willing to pay.

Needless to say, financial disaster could await serious collectors who don't take the appraisal of their collection seriously. With the high transparency and fluidity of the wine market, collectors should also be concerned with updating their appraisals frequently. And, wine collections, more so most other types, constantly change through buying, selling, and drinking. So, a systematic inventory system, not unlike one used for art collection, is essential to knowing, at any time, the value of the overall collection.

Serious Risk Management for Serious Wine Collectors

As with any activity that increases financial exposure, collecting valuable or rare wines requires special attention to managing the risks involved. And yes, there is special coverage for wine collections that goes far beyond the protections a standard homeowners policy can provide. At a relatively low cost—about 45 to 50 cents per $100—it's one of the bigger no-brainers in risk management.

Essentially, there are two types of coverage—a blanket policy and a standalone policy, both available only from a specialty insurer.

1. *Blanket policy:* This coverage provides blanket protection over your entire collection. If you're collection consists primarily of lower-value wines—below $1,000—this could be the best solution. The insured amount is a lump sum and doesn't require documentation; however, it would be important to hire a qualified appraiser to itemize the collection if for no other reason than to determine whether a blanket policy is the best solution. If you do happen to have a higher-value wine, say $25,000, your blanket policy may only cover your loss up to $10,000 for any one bottle.

2. *Standalone policy:* If your collection is full of high-value and rare wines, you shouldn't settle for anything less than a standalone policy that insures your wines individually. Of course, this requires individual documentation, but it will cover your expensive wines up to 150 percent of their original cost. However, it is the responsibility of the collector to track and then inform the insurer of any significant increase in value. Most collectors use a combination of blanket and standalone policies, which is a more practical solution when a collection has a large quantity of lower- and higher-value wines.

It is important to note that wine insurance is highly specialized and that no two policies are alike. As such, you will find variations in the type and scope of coverage. At a minimum, you should look for a policy with the following features:

- Zero deductibility.
- Full coverage for theft and fire.
- Full coverage for loss due to mechanical breakdown caused by fire or lightning (mechanical breakdown due to poor maintenance is not covered).
- At least partial coverage for spoilage caused by failure of refrigeration equipment.
- Coverage for accidental breakage (fewer insurers provide this).
- Coverage for wine housed in storage facilities.
- Coverage for shipping.

THEN THERE'S THE ANTIQUES, RUGS, CHINA, AND OTHER TREASURES

As you can see by now, managing the risks of all the various types of treasures one can accumulate follows the same essential pattern. Anything of high value, especially rare items, need their own schedules; expert appraisals; inventories with documentation; value tracking; loss prevention measures; review and update. Rinse and repeat. A house full of antique furnishings, rare china, furs, and other treasures accumulated over time can hold hundreds of thousands or even millions of dollars of potential losses. While it's true that, except for the rare and one-of-kind piece, almost anything is replaceable, trying to replace a couple of million dollars' worth of antique or custom furnishings with the insurance proceeds of a standard contents endorsement or blanket coverage would be a significant financial setback for anyone.

Once more, for final edification, high-value items and collections, including artwork, jewelry, antique furnishings, furs, china, and any other treasures of value, need to be actively managed in order to optimally reduce your financial exposure.

- Have all valuables, including lower-value items, independently appraised. Should a lower-value antique be destroyed in a fire, you'll need proof of value in order to collect on the insurance coverage.
- Maintain an accurate inventory of all valuables to include descriptions, current appraisal, documentation, and photos or videos. Inventory data should be stored in a secure location.
- Buy worldwide, all-risk coverage.
- Keep your insurer up-to-date with any acquisitions or sales. With specialty coverage, new pieces are covered for up to 90 days.
- Utilize a collection management system that can track inventory.

Rinse and repeat.

The essence of the risk management process is determining an individual's threshold for financial loss where it becomes necessary to transfer all or a part of the exposure to an insurance company. Essentially, there are three reasons why people decide to transfer the risk and buy insurance:

1. They can't bear the thought of being without it.
2. They can't afford the loss or to replace it.
3. They value the convenience of simply submitting a claim for a lost or damaged item.

As it relates to high-value items, whether it's fine art, wine, or jewelry, the risk management process must include expert appraisals, a collection management system, and specialized insurance coverage.

CHAPTER 4

The Hired Help—Who's Watching Whom?

I t so happens that many of my clients are Jimmy Buffet fans, as am I. But, I wonder if they ever considered the lyrics of his song Gypsies In The Palace as they packed their bags to take their families on a month-long vacation to Europe. Of course, I'm not implying that they need to be concerned with their household staff raiding the liquor cabinet and swinging from the chandeliers. However, metaphorically, the song does raise the unsettling issue of just who is watching the hired help when you're not looking. Although most high net worth families would like to believe that their longtime house manager or upstairs maid are staunchly loyal and beyond personal reproach, the unsettling facts reveal that domestic employees can be the family's most exposed point of vulnerability. To be sure, in nearly all criminal or civil cases involving domestic employees, the domestic employer didn't see it coming, and most wouldn't have believed it would happen to them.

THE REAL RISK OF "NANNY REVENGE"

If you aren't interested in California politics, you may not have heard this story about the maid who brought down a gubernatorial candidate. But since it also involved the publicity-seeking attorney, Gloria Allred, you probably did. It was the 2010 gubernatorial race, which pitted former governor Jerry Brown against political upstart and billionaire, Meg Whitman, also the former CEO of eBay. Whitman was also staunchly anti–illegal immigration. The polls were very close, and in fact, Whitman had been building momentum when Allred, a Jerry Brown supporter, struck.

With the cameras and lights she so desperately covets, Allred paraded before the press the former and now disgruntled maid of Meg Whitman. Apparently, Whitman had hired the maid 10 years earlier based on false documents she had presented—a fake driver's license and Social Security card. Allred alleged that Whitman retained the maid even after finding out she was in the country illegally; and then she only let her go to protect her candidacy. The maid alleged that Whitman still owed her money.

As it turned out, the maid was here illegally, and there was no proof that Whitman knew about it. Whitman offered to pay her former maid what she thought she was owed, and then went back to campaigning. During the next week, all of the Hispanic interest groups screamed "Hypocrite!" and Whitman took a nosedive in the polls. She ultimately lost by double digits.

Why do I highlight this story? No one broke the law. No one was sued. I refer to it as a perfect illustration of how the mere accusation of wrongful action in a domestic staff situation can damage the reputation of a high-profile person. And there are plenty more examples where "nanny revenge" has traumatized a former employer. By the way, another (former) California governor had his reputation slimed when a former maid threatened to reveal to the world the existence of the governor's illegitimate son—but I really didn't want to go down *that* road.

WHAT CAN GO WRONG? EVERYTHING

In the real world, cases of domestic staff disputes can and do involve civil or criminal charges of discrimination, sexual harassment, or wrongful termination, resulting in fines and monetary settlements. There are also countless cases involving the hiring of unauthorized aliens. A domestic employer can be subject to legal penalties ranging from criminal fines up to and including imprisonment. At the other extreme, there are the tragic cases involving more heinous acts by domestic employees that, while very rare, should give domestic employers pause as they consider their hiring and vetting process.

Unquestionably, the hiring of domestic employees—be they nannies, butlers, house managers, or personal assistants—is a high-risk proposition; yet, too often the hiring and vetting process is taken for granted. Worse yet, too many high net worth people fail to operate the management of their household as the business that it really is, leaving themselves open to any number of liability risks. Chief among these risks are inviting a dishonest or dangerous person into the household, being subjected to a lawsuit from a disgruntled employee, and being charged with a workers compensation claim.

In my own files I can count dozens of claims of all varieties that were filed against high net worth clients who didn't see them coming. Here are four, right off the top:

1. A high-profile client sued his former nanny after she went before cameras to talk about their private lives. The nanny then turned around and countersued, alleging mistreatment by her former employer.
2. A professional athlete had nearly $500,000 stolen from him by his personal assistant, who was charged with depositing forged checks into her checking account.
3. A former housekeeper pilfered 430 bottles of wine, worth $200,000, from her employer's rare wine collection.
4. A client's insurance carrier settled a dog-bite claim for $2 million. Why so much? Because the domestic worker had been bitten before and his employer convinced him not to tell the emergency room doctor that it was the family dog that bit him. After the second, more serious bite, the worker went for the big bucks.

Too often, high net worth people who hire domestic workers fail to understand that their legal obligations as employers start the minute their employees are hired. Failure to understand the employer–employee relationship can expose all family members to personal litigation and even danger. It is not at all uncommon for families to begin treating longtime household workers as "family," often disregarding the formality and legality of the employer–employee relationship. And that can only heighten their risk exposure. Just ask Meg Whitman.

MANAGING THE RISKS OF HOUSEHOLD STAFF

Of course, as with most other risks and liabilities associated with a wealthy lifestyle, there are insurance solutions that can transfer the financial risk. But, insurance won't always be able to help domestic employers who are victims of some criminal activities; or if it is discovered that an employee is an undocumented worker; or if other employment laws are broken. When it comes to managing the risks associated with domestic employees, prevention is the most effective solution. And that begins before the search for a new employee even begins.

Many of my clients have run their own business at one time or another and I can't imagine their hiring a new employee without having a complete job description that lists duties, responsibilities, and expectations. Nor would they ever bring someone on board unless there were clear performance measures and a scheduled review process with established conditions for termination. And what CEO or business owner would hire anyone who hasn't undergone a comprehensive background check? So, you can imagine my astonishment at the number of them who don't apply the same level of diligence to their most important business—the running of their household.

I've come across domestic employers who couldn't answer some of most basic questions about their employment practices, such as:

- Do you know if you're in compliance with all federal and state requirements in your hiring practices?
- Do you conduct a thorough online and offline background investigation on each employee?
- Do you know the sources of your prospective employees?
- Are you certain that you are following immigration rules?
- Have you taken steps to protect financial data?
- Are you properly following payroll tax requirements?

A "no" answer to any one of these questions will almost certainly lead to some very serious consequences. More than one "no" will almost certainly invite disaster. Any businessperson knows that no company could survive under such operational ineptitude. So, why would you invite a similar disaster into your home? The answer is that you wouldn't—at least not intentionally.

One would think that with the economic downturn, the demand for domestic workers would have subsided. But in fact just the opposite is true. Since 2009, the market for domestic workers has exploded, with the biggest demand from newly affluent households. These tend to be households led by couples who spend more than half their time pursuing their careers, requiring at least part-time care for their children and their homes. The settings are often informal, so the need for strict procedures and manuals might seem unnecessary. And those who do look into the logistics of hiring help might just skip them due to the "hassle factor."

Whatever the reason, the growth of domestic hiring among the newly affluent and even the newly wealthy has created a significant knowledge gap in hiring and employment practices. The ultra-wealthy can rely on their Family Office, many of which are well-versed in domestic employment risk and liabilities. But even with them, the buck stops with the domestic employers, so they need to have at least a rudimentary knowledge of employee law. The affluent and wealthy can certainly outsource the tasks of screening and hiring to staffing agencies; however, the responsibility for adherence to the law before and during employment still falls squarely on the shoulders of their employer(s).

FOUR THINGS ALL DOMESTIC EMPLOYERS NEED TO KNOW ABOUT EMPLOYEE LAW

When a domestic employer is in a hiring mode, he or she must be able to wade through many layers of regulations born out of a tangled web of federal, state, and even local jurisdictions. Mismanaged hiring or employment practices, whether intentional or unintentional, can have costly consequences, so domestic employers are wisely cautioned to know how employee law applies to them.

1. **Know which laws apply to you.**

   Various state and federal employment laws are applied on the basis of the type, size, and scope of an employer. For instance, some federal laws, such as the Americans with Disabilities Act, apply to businesses that employ at least 15 employees, while the Equal Pay Act applies to any employer who falls within the purview of the Fair Labor Standards Act, which includes just about every employer.

2. **Know your state's requirements.**

   Most states have issued their own requirements for laws that regulate discrimination, so it is just a matter of studying the regulations for the state in which the employer operates. For some regulations, such as those that regulate wages and overtime, state and federal laws overlap. This requires an employer to comply with both sets of laws, even where the standards are different. Local governments may issue their own wage requirements, which can add another layer of compliance.

3. **Know that multi-state employment compounds the complexity.**

   The challenge of complying with overlapping federal, state, and local laws is compounded if the employer employs people in multiple states. Each state may have its own requirements, and the mix of government regulations in one state may require a completely different approach to total compliance than with another state. The solution for some employers is to adopt the highest possible standards for discrimination, wages, and such, and apply those in all states. This also could address the difficult issue of creating employee handbooks that can satisfy each state and locality's standards.

4. **Know the requirements for conducting a valid background check.**

   Background checks are becoming more necessary, and employers are coming under more scrutiny in their practices. The Fair Credit Reporting Act regulates the practice of background checks, and its requirements can be somewhat confusing. While employers have the right to check into the background of prospective employees, the prospective employees also have rights, which are enumerated in the Act.

Employee laws have sprung up piecemeal over the course of many decades to the point where all employers are impacted in one way or another. Understanding the laws that affect you as a domestic employer is vital to minimize legal mishaps. The best course of action for any domestic employer is to work with an employment attorney who can help structure practices and policies for employee hiring and relations.

A Word about Nanny-Cams

After a thorough background investigation, my client, who lives in Connecticut, hired a nanny to care for his two children, ages two and four. With an impeccable employment history, she seemed to be everything he was looking for—smart, caring, and knowledgeable in CPR and other emergency procedures. In fact, she seemed too good to be true. Not one to leave anything to chance, and being somewhat of a technology buff, my client installed a series of hidden cameras throughout the house linked to his computer so that he could check on his children from anywhere in the world.

From a hotel room in London, he logged in to check up on things, as he did several times daily. The video is streamed live, but he can also play back recorded video by entering the day and the hour he wants to view. On this day he went back to the time at which his wife left for work the prior day, and he saw something that made him seethe with anger. The nanny had placed both children in the play crib, so she could watch *Good Morning America* without interruption.

First, the older child doesn't belong in a crib; and as he tried to climb out, the nanny threatened punishment if he didn't stay put. Second, as she lay on the sofa to watch her show, the four-year-old began to take out his frustration on his little sister, hitting her with one of her stuffed animals. The nanny, who was only allowed to watch television during the children's naptime, simply turned up the volume on the television.

After confronting the nanny with the videotape, they fired her for breaching the rules and putting their children in danger. She later brought suit claiming the video was an illegal invasion of her privacy. The court ruled that a video-only recording within the home is perfectly legal at any time without informing anyone. The problem for my client is that the video included a sound recording, and in Connecticut, recording someone's voice without their permission is illegal.

Bottom-line: Nanny-cams are okay; just turn off the sound, and be sure to check the appendix for your state's specific laws on recording laws.

WORKERS COMPENSATION, EMPLOYEE BENEFITS, AND THE EMPLOYMENT PRACTICES ISSUES DOMESTIC STAFF PRESENT

The first mistake many domestic employers make is not treating their relationship with domestic workers as an employment arrangement. Instead, they treat it as an independent contract arrangement. Whether it is out of ignorance or simply an attempt to skirt employment laws, domestic employers leave themselves open to costly fines and lawsuits. Domestic employers discovered this the hard way when the last recession drove many domestic workers to the unemployment lines, but they weren't eligible for benefits because their employers hired them under the radar. However, the biggest lawsuits are reserved for employers who fail to adhere to Workers Compensation laws or fair employment practices as dictated by federal law.

Employee versus Contractor

As a way to avoid the "hassle factor" or out of ignorance, some families choose to hire their domestic workers as independent contractors, or as 1099 employees, believing that this arrangement will shift the burden of paying for taxes and insurance to the "self-employed" worker. Unfortunately, the decision about which kind of arrangement they can use is not up to the family; rather it is defined by law based on the nature of the relationship. Only in rare cases does a domestic worker qualify as an independent contractor. The key determinants are the level of independence and authority the employee has in performing his duties, and whether the worker is "self-contained," that is, he uses his own equipment, provides his own insurance, and stands to make a profit or loss on the work performed.

If, as most do, the worker falls within the category of "employee," then the domestic employer is subject to all of the federal and state laws guiding hiring and employment, including payroll taxes, Workers Compensation, and Fair Employment Practices.

Remarkably, the IRS reports that as many as 90 percent of domestic employers improperly file their employees' taxes, subjecting themselves to fines and audit risk.[5] Again, whether this is born of ignorance or hassle avoidance, domestic employers need to know that they are increasingly being targeted by state and federal agencies tasked with protecting the rights of domestic workers as well as bringing employers into compliance with all employment laws.

Essentially, any employee who earns more than $1,700 in a year must be reported to the IRS and registered for Federal Insurance Contributions Act (FICA) payments. These payments, which amount to 15.3 percent of an employee's current wages, are required contributions to Social Security and Medicare. Half is paid by the employer and the other half is deducted from the employee's wages.

Of course, once an employee is on the IRS radar, the employer becomes visible to other federal and state agencies that have their own requirements. One such requirement is compulsory payments into the state's Unemployment Insurance based on a certain amount of wages (typically

around $1,000) paid to an employee. Unemployment Insurance require-
ments vary by state.

Workers Compensation

A domestic employer's biggest exposure is in the area of personal injury.
While homeowners liability coverage may suffice for a nonemployee incident, if the injury occurs in the normal course of employment, the policy
may limit the amount available to the injured employee. Also, claims for
lost wages are not typically covered under a homeowner's liability coverage.

Domestic employers can face substantial penalties and liabilities for
failure to comply with federal and state requirements, but particularly for
failing to comply with compulsory Workers Compensation laws. Many
domestic employers are under the mistaken impression that their homeowners policy will cover costs associated with injuries sustained by domestic
employees. While some homeowners policies can include an endorsement
for this coverage, it varies by state and insurer. Workers Compensation
requirements vary by state—it's compulsory in many states and voluntary
in others—but it generally covers employees who work a certain number of
hours per week. In the state of New York, the law covers employees regardless of the number of hours they work.

Employees who are not protected by Workers Compensation retain the
common-law right to sue the employer for injury damages. The employer's
only defense is that the employee was engaged in some sort of illegal or
improper activity. In states that require Workers Compensation coverage,
the liability portion of a homeowners policy will only cover employers if an
employee is injured in a nonbusiness activity, and domestic employee activities are considered business-related.

In most states, domestic employers have strict legal responsibilities,
which is why some choose to rely on reputable domestic-staffing agencies
to provide licensed and bonded workers, as well as to manage their wages,
payroll, taxes, and insurance. Domestic employers who choose to do it themselves will typically outsource the payroll administration to payroll prepar-
ers and the Workers Compensation issue to a risk management service.

Employment Practices Liability Insurance (EPLI)

Aside from the risk of hiring dishonest workers, domestic employers are
extremely vulnerable to lawsuits stemming from unfair or discrimina-
tory employment practices. How many times have we heard the story of a
domestic employer's sexual advances being rebuffed by a household worker
who is then targeted with unreasonable work demands or intimidation by

an embarrassed or angered employer? Sexual harassment lawsuits are notoriously prevalent in domestic employment situations. How about the stories of a domestic employer who is overheard by a household worker making a disparaging remark about her own ethnicity? Even in the best of employer–employee relationships, the worker would have every right to sue the employer.

In this day of extreme litigiousness, an employment practice lawsuit could come from anyone at any time based on nothing more than an innocent joke, a misinterpreted gesture, or a termination gone awry. It's not enough to ensure that the employer–employee demarcation be maintained at all times; domestic employers must also assume that they will someday be the target of a lawsuit and take all precautionary measures to guard against it. Considering the exposure a domestic employer has, especially when employing multiple workers, the most commonsense solution would be Employment Practices Liability Insurance (EPLI).

EPLI can be purchased as an add-on to some personal or excess liability policies, and it generally provides high limits and broad coverage for incidences of unfair employment practices. The coverage includes payments for legal defense costs, with a limit of at least $1 million. The coverage applies to household staff, including butlers, chauffeurs, cooks, housekeepers, nannies, personal assistants and other employed household staff.

Most EPLI policies also provide $25,000 or more of coverage for reputational injury. Some carriers can provide risk management services, including crisis management and reputation repair. The high-end risk management firms will consult with domestic employers on a full range of preventative measures to mitigate the risks associated with hiring and employing domestic workers.

CHAPTER 5

Which Car Will I Drive Today, the Ferrari or the Bentley?

Nearly three months after Superstorm *Sandy* slammed into New York, New Jersey, and Connecticut, thousands of stranded homeowners were still up in the air, and thousands more were still without power in the midst of one of the coldest winters on record. So it may seem a bit trivial to point out that the storm also wiped out thousands of luxury and classic cars that lined the waterfronts of this tri-state area. While the dollar amount of damages pales in comparison to the loss of homes, estimates for luxury and classic car damages alone put the total at somewhere between $300 million and $500 million, which is not a trivial amount.[6]

While it's not the first hurricane to target concentrated areas of population, *Sandy*, with its massive tidal surge, was the worst kind of storm for cars in general. In addition to the typical falling tree branches and collapsing garages, most cars suffered from the massive flooding. Salt water is among a car's worst enemies. And for luxury and classic cars, every custom part or material begins to corrode almost immediately. The most tragic losses were the prized collectible autos that can't be replaced.

IT'S NOT YOUR OLDSMOBILE'S INSURANCE COVERAGE

Events like *Sandy*, while rare, are stark testaments to the importance of matching your insurance coverage to your particular needs. While there is no telling how many of the thousands of luxury cars were underinsured relative to their value, the fact is that many luxury car owners often find themselves on the short end when it is time to repair or replace their high-end vehicles. The biggest losers in these kinds of events are classic car owners and collectors. Without specialized coverage, their insurers see nothing but an old car and a low *Blue Book* price.

Book Value versus Stated Value versus Agreed Value

At issue for owners of classics and collectibles, or even mainstream cars that have been souped-up, is the actual cost of repairing or replacing their damaged cars. For some, especially those with one-of-kind treasures, replacement is probably out of the question. Because parts for many of these types of cars are rare, their costs can actually increase over time; in many cases, the cost of repairs can exceed the original price of the car. At the very least, the cost of repairs can easily exceed the book value of the car.

The first mistake classic car owners often make is to simply tack their specialty car onto their standard auto policy, which pays the cost of repairs or the market value of the vehicle, whichever is less. Specialized cars need specialized insurance, and, in the realm of classic cars or customized luxury cars, the best course is to go with a specialized carrier. Even then it is important to know exactly what you are getting, because some carriers will offer *stated value* policies, which might suffice in some cases, and others offer *agreed value* policies, which provide the ultimate coverage for high-end vehicles.

Stated Value Policies

Stated value policies pay for repair costs or the stated value of the car, whichever is less at the time of the claim. The stated value is the number provided to the insurer in order to determine the amount of the premium. If a higher value is stated, a higher premium is charged. Even though the insurer accepts the stated value at the time of policy issue, it is under no formal obligation to adhere to the stated value in the event of a claim. Based on the language in the policy, the insurer could, instead, establish an *actual cash value* if it is a lesser sum.

Agreed Value Policies

Agreed value establishes and guarantees a specific amount of coverage at the time of policy issue. Instead of allowing the insurer to establish a value, either stated or actual, agreed value provides for an appraisal of the vehicle that will be accepted by both parties as a valid representation of its worth. And, unlike standard insurance policies, agreed value means that the value of your car does not depreciate.

Generally, in order to secure agreed value, you may have to agree to some driving limitations (i.e., weekend leisure driving only). But if the vehicle is well-maintained and protected with added security features, insurers may loosen some of the restrictions.

Obviously, agreed value is the best possible coverage for classic and specialty car owners, but it is important to be able to negotiate the agreed value from a position of knowledge. Specialty insurers not only offer the unique insurance products needed, they also are more apt to appreciate the vehicle's intrinsic value and negotiate in good faith.

Insuring the Other Car

With your perfectly restored, classic 1970 Plymouth Barracuda with its 426 Hemi V8 nestled safely in the garage following the weekend, you're ready to pull out your Audi R8 Quattro or Mercedes CL600 for your week-day commute. The good news is that insuring your luxury car doesn't have to be any more difficult than insuring any mainstream vehicle. Of course, you need the highest liability limits you can get along with comprehensive and collision coverage for damage to your vehicle; and therein may lie the problem, as many standard insurance companies won't write policies for *high-performance* cars. And, for those who will, you can expect to pay substantially more if you have a blemish or two on your driving record.

HOW MUCH DO YOU KNOW ABOUT AUTO INSURANCE?

In a 2013 knowledge survey conducted by Insurance.com, 500 drivers were asked 10 multiple-choice questions about automobile insurance basics.[7] When asked about basic insurance terminology and insurance purchase practices, the entire group scored an average of 32 percent. Only 2 percent knew the definition of comprehensive coverage and 7 percent were able to identify the typical premium discounts available from most carriers.

Remarkably, the respondents who said that they have actually read their policies scored 28 percent, while those who admitted to not having read them scored 35 percent. And those who claimed to be very knowledgeable in auto insurance matters scored just 26 percent.

The knowledge survey is a clear indication that drivers of all ages, genders, and incomes are likely to be making big mistakes when purchasing their auto insurance policies, especially if they try to buy them directly online. This makes the strongest case yet for the value in working with a knowledgeable insurance broker who understands your specific auto insurance needs.

If there is one glaring mistake many high-end car owners make, it's setting their deductibles too low. Perhaps they figure that if they have to pay such high premiums, anyway, they should try to get the most out of their coverage. But considering that most high-end car owners are probably able to fully self-insure their cars, except for the liability coverage; wouldn't it make sense to increase the deductible to a level that could save thousands of dollars in premiums over the long term? Of course, that's a personal choice.

INSURING FOR THE UNDERINSURED AND UNINSURED

It seems remarkable that more than one in seven drivers in the United States is uninsured. But with the slumping economy, that number is expected to increase. And that doesn't account for the millions more who can only afford to buy the minimum liability coverage that is required by state law. Needless to say, the chances of being hit by someone who doesn't have the means to fix or replace your car or pay liability claims are surprisingly high. The chances are even greater when you consider that high-end cars are sometimes targeted by uninsured motorists looking for a score.

Although most states have mandatory liability insurance requirements, one in six drivers still manages to roam the streets without owning any insurance. The even larger problem is the number of drivers who purchase only the minimum liability coverage, of which there are tens of millions. These are all financial time bombs ready to explode at the moment they strike your car.

For instance, in California, the minimum liability limits are 30/60/15: $30,000 for bodily injury coverage per person up to $60,000 total per accident and $15,000 of property damage per accident. You're driving your business colleagues in your Jaguar XK8 one evening and a driver with these minimum liability limits runs a red light and rams your passenger side at 40 miles per hour. Your passengers sustain serious injuries and must be airlifted to a hospital. You suffer a broken collar bone and cuts when the front and side airbags are deployed. Your $80,000 Jaguar is a total loss.

Your passengers both suffer spinal injuries that will require extensive treatment and rehabilitation after they undergo surgery. Their medical bills will exceed $300,000, and your medical costs will come in at $20,000 for total bodily injuries of $320,000. Your Jaguar is headed for the scrap heap but your outstanding loan of $55,000 lives on. The at-fault driver's insurer will cover $60,000 for the bodily injury costs and $15,000 for personal property, leaving you with a $260,000 bodily injury liability and $40,000 outstanding balance on your auto loan. Your liability would be even greater in many states that have even lower minimum liability limit requirements.

The good news is that most high-end car owners recognize the risk of uninsured and underinsured motorists, so they tend to purchase the maximum liability coverage along with what is offered for UM/UIM (uninsured motorist/underinsured motorist) coverage. While high-end car drivers would never turn down UM/UIM coverage, many don't give enough thought to how their UM/UIM coverage protects them. For instance, most people are unaware of the fact that UM/UIM coverage can protect them in or out of their cars. How does this coverage work? Following are a few examples.

Example 1:

Insured's Bodily Injury Damages	$300,000
Insured's Liability Limit	$500,000
Insured's UM/UIM Limit	$250,000
Other Motor Vehicle Liability Limit	$ 25,000

Outcome: The insured (you) purchased the maximum UM/UIM coverage offered by your insurance company. You will recover $25,000 from the negligent owner or operator of the other motor vehicle and $225,000 ($250,000 less $25,000) from the UM/UIM coverage, for a total recovery of $250,000.

Example 2:

Insured's Bodily Injury Damages	$100,000
Insured's Liability Limit	$ 25,000
Insured's UM/UIM Limit	$ 25,000
Other Motor Vehicle Liability Limit	$ 25,000

Outcome: You will recover $25,000 from the negligent owner or operator of the other motor vehicle. You will receive nothing under your UM/UIM coverage since the other owner or operator's vehicle did not have less liability insurance than your vehicle. If your liability and UM/UIM limits were both $50,000, you would collect another $25,000 in UM/UIM from your insurer.

Example 3:

Insured's Bodily Injury Damages	$ 60,000
Insured's Liability Limit	$100,000
Insured's UM/UIM Limit	$100,000
Other Motor Vehicle Liability Limit	$ 50,000

Outcome: The insured (you) would recover $50,000 from the other negligent motor vehicle owner or operator and $10,000 under the UM/UIM coverage (the difference between the amount of your UM/UIM coverage and the liability coverage available from the other motor vehicle owner or operator, limited by the amount of your bodily injury damages).

Example 4:

Insured's Bodily Injury Damages	$150,000
Insured's Liability Limit	$100,000
Insured's UM/UIM Limit	$100,000
Other Motor Vehicle Liability Limit	$ 25,000

Outcome: What if you and the other motor vehicle owner or operator were each 50 percent at fault for the accident? Your total recovery
would then be $75,000, in light of comparative negligence of the parties
involved in the accident. The insured (you) would recover $25,000 from
the other negligent motor vehicle owner or operator and $50,000 under
the UM/UIM coverage.

What if the other motor vehicle owner or operator was totally at fault
for the accident? Your recovery would then be $25,000, from the other
negligent motor vehicle owner or operator and $75,000 under your UM/
UIM coverage. Had higher liability and UM/UIM liability been purchased
of $150,000 or more, the UM/UIM recovery would then be $125,000.

It's highly recommended that high net worth drivers purchase the maximum UM/UIM coverage available and have it attach at the proper limit to
their own personal umbrella liability coverage. Insurance companies specializing in the high net worth client have the ability to provide UM/UIM limits
as a rider to the personal umbrella policy providing expanded protection
for you and your family. The additional annual premium usually amounts
to less than a tank of gas.

"It Was Fun-Fun-Fun Till Her Daddy Took the T-Bird Away"

The iconic Beach Boys song may be a half-century old, but the image of a
teenager taking her daddy's car to hamburger stand instead of the library
still plays out in towns across America. Since the invention of the automobile, it has become a cultural mandate for cars to figure prominently, almost
obsessively, in the lives of teenagers. But, as any insurance claims adjuster
will tell you, teenagers and cars are like butane near an open flame. With
an accident rate several times that of the average driver, teenagers are risk
multipliers who sit high on the radar of insurance companies, which is why
this particular rite of passage can be costly.

Of course, paying high premiums for teenage drivers is not unique to
high net worth families; all families must add their driving-aged children
to their auto insurance policies. While they may be in a better position to
afford the additional cost, high net worth families need to be concerned
with liability limits, purchasing the maximum amounts available to protect
their greater exposure. While increased liability limits don't usually increase

premium costs substantially, the collision and comprehensive coverage for high-end or luxury cars can increase significantly.

If you have one particular car assigned to your teenager, or purchase a separate car, the premium rate is largely determined based on the type of car he or she will be driving. High-end cars, especially those with powerful engines, will obviously rate the highest on the premium scale, while bigger and less powerful cars (i.e., Toyota Camry) will rate the lowest. Insurers figure that if a teenager drives a car with a powerful engine, he is likely to test its power frequently. Your insurer can recommend cars with the lowest insurance rates. Regardless, it is almost always less expensive to add your teenagers to your auto insurance policy than it is to buy a separate policy (in those states where it is allowed).

The good news is that insurers are willing to reward good behavior by offering discounts for good report cards and an unblemished driving record (after a period of driving). Many companies also offer a discount when your teenager completes a driver safety course. Another way to earn a discount is to have your insurer install a monitoring system that will track your teen's driving behavior—speeds, braking, turns, seatbelts, and so on. Some systems will even give your teen immediate feedback if her driving is out of line.

The Other Drivers

Remember the domestic staff from the prior chapter? Yes, many of the high-net-worth also allow these employees access to their vehicles. Whether it is the Nanny doing school pickup and drop off or the personal assistant borrowing your car to run an errand these other drivers present a risk as they use your vehicle.

Personal risk management and protecting you and your family starts prior to the date of hire. As part of the screening process obtain permission from potential domestic staff to review their motor vehicle records. The last thing you want to see is a Nanny with a history of driving while intoxicated (DWI) offenses! In addition, many insurers want to know about staff members with access to your vehicles. Again, consult with your insurance representative about the best action to take to be certain your coverage is adequate and includes the domestic employees accessing your vehicles.

HIGH-END CARS NEED HIGH-END INSURANCE COVERAGE

Sometimes your best bet is to work with the same specialty insurer that covers your specialty car. The advantages in doing so are multifold. First, your insurer will have a better understanding of your vehicle use, which could translate into broader coverage. Second, you can achieve greater efficiency by using one carrier with one policy and one bill. And, of course, you stand to benefit from multicar pricing. Everyone likes a discount. If you don't have a specialty car in the garage, it would still be important to work with an insurer that specializes in high-end luxury vehicles.

Of course, you pay more for the best possible coverage, but, as a sophisticated consumer who appreciates the value of your cars, you also appreciate value in superior insurance coverage that fully protects your investment as well as your assets. Most high-end automobile consumers value coverage and service more than price. In the end, they want a high-end insurance program just as they want a high-end car. But, what should you expect from a high-end insurance program?

Service, Service, Service

Above all else, high-end car owners value service, the more "white glove" the better, and why not? Paying thousands of dollars a year in premiums should get you to the concierge level in any insurance program. You should expect a much higher level of service and expertise. You don't need an insurance salesperson; you need a consultant who can conjure up innovative coverages, and a true advocate dedicated to your file. When you have a claim, your number should be first on their speed-dial. And you shouldn't have to chase your insurer down for coverage upgrades, such as deductible reductions for good driving behavior. At a minimum, your insurance concierge service should include the following:

- *Your choice of repair shop:* None of this working with a shop in the insurer's network. You should be able to take your car to your longtime mechanic, or to any body shop he recommends.
- *Rental car service:* If you drive a Bentley, should you really have to settle for a Toyota Camry as a rental replacement? Work with an insurer who will provide a like-kind rental replacement and who will deliver it to you.
- *Prompt claim response:* Your carrier should provide prompt (within 12 hours) claims processing, which includes an expert damage appraiser and a payment for covered damage.

For high-end car owners who understand that their affection for luxury comes at a cost, paying higher insurance premiums should not be a burden; however, the expectation for high-end service and attention is not the least bit unreasonable.

CHAPTER 6

How Big Is Your Umbrella?

Since I am on the topic of high-end cars for high net worth people, it's as good a time as any to revisit the critical importance of personal umbrella liability coverage. The costs associated with fixing or replacing even the most exotic car pale in comparison to the amount of money wealthy people will shell out to pay liability claims. It's no coincidence that jury awards and settlements grow in proportion to a person's net worth. Such is the mindset of our society today: What's yours is mine if you're dumb enough to leave yourself open for me to take it. While that may seem like a harsh commentary on society, it's a game that plays itself out thousands of times each year, and the stakes run into the tens of billions of dollars.

Consider this actual case: Timothy and Clara have a net worth of $10 million. In addition to a broad coverage auto insurance policy for their Mercedes CL600, they also have a $1 million personal umbrella liability policy. Coming out of a turn on a rainy night their car swerved into an oncoming car, seriously injuring a family of five. A jury finds the couple at fault and awards each of the family members $500,000 for lifelong pain and suffering, as well as economic damages. In addition to legal fees and the cost of replacing the family's totaled vehicle, the total cost is more than $3 million.

Fortunately, the father was only injured. Had he died, the jury may have determined that his $100,000 income, now lost to the family, is worth an amount equivalent to the number of working years he lost—perhaps another $3 million.

While Timothy and Clara had the right kind of auto insurance with the highest liability limits, and a $1 million umbrella policy they thought was enough, their total exposure for an accident they never envisioned happening could have been more than half of their net worth. Had both the father and the mother died, the total claims could have taken everything they had.

Now, let's reverse the roles. Timothy and Clara are driving with their two kids on a rainy night, and, out of the corner of his eye, Timothy catches the glaring headlights of a car bearing down on them as they enter an intersection. The impact was at full speed, but luckily the extra safety features of their Mercedes CL600 saved their lives. Their injuries, however, were severe and would require hundreds of thousands of dollars in medical treatments. The driver of the other car was critically injured and was eventually booked for DUI. And, as bad luck would have it, he was uninsured.

Timothy's auto coverage included the maximum $250,000/500,000 coverage for uninsured motorists. He also carried a $1 million umbrella policy, so, naturally, he thought the extra liability protection would cover their medical costs. Unfortunately, his personal umbrella liability coverage did not extend to uninsured motorists.

Most wealthy people are finally getting it, and they are arming themselves with personal liability umbrella policies. And just as they do with their homeowner's risks, high net worth people tend to drastically underestimate their personal liability risks. Also, just as there are big differences between standard homeowners coverage and coverage for high-end customized homes, there are some significant differences between standard umbrella policies and the specialized umbrella policies that better serve the wealthy.

STANDARD UMBRELLA POLICIES VERSUS SPECIALIZED UMBRELLA POLICIES

For the wealthy, that level of coverage, and the need to constantly update their personal liability coverage, rules out working with most traditional property and casualty insurers. Most don't offer the high limits needed, and generally, they aren't equipped to personally assist high net worth people assess their actual financial risks. Only specialized insurers have the product, the expertise, and the services to provide the appropriate level of coverage while working with their clients to lower their exposure through risk mitigation measures.

With most standard umbrella policies, the insurer requires that you have all of your property and casualty coverage with them, as well. That may be fine for people with minimal risk exposures, but for high net worth people, it can be severely limiting. Not only will it limit the amount of coverage available, the coverage itself may have quite a few gaps. For example, standard umbrella policies typically protect only those assets held in the insured's name. Assets held in trust or in any other form of ownership may still be exposed. Only a specialized umbrella policy can enumerate the various asset titles to ensure they are covered under the umbrella.

HOW MUCH IS ENOUGH?

In determining how much personal liability coverage they should have, most people with umbrella policies tend to think in terms of what is available. For instance, when working through a traditional property and casualty agent, mainstream carriers may limit personal liability coverage to between $1 million and $2 million. While some carriers offer higher limits, typically up to $5 million, you usually need to jump through a lot of hoops to obtain it. The "hassle factor" drives most people to simply avoid it.

Like most other types of insurance, the $1 million umbrella policy has become commoditized. For the "measly" $200 in premium, insurance agents can almost shame their clients into getting one. So it typically becomes an add-on to other coverages their clients buy. And high net worth people are not immune to this pitch. What the agents might not tell their clients is that this could easily increase their coverage, at a cost of around $100 per million to a high of $100 million. But they would rather write the $1 million umbrella policy than have to refer their high net worth clients to a specialized insurer.

While I don't subscribe to general rules-of-thumb for something as critical as risk protection, which requires a thorough assessment, here are some general guidelines to use as a starting point:

- Everyone should own a $1 million personal umbrella policy at a minimum.
- If you have any assets and high earning potential, you should buy no less than $2 million of coverage.
- If you consider yourself affluent, you should have at minimum between $5 million and $10 million of coverage.
- You should always buy at least $1 million more than you think you need.

High net worth people need to, instead, think in terms of their actual financial exposure. The easiest rule-of-thumb is that your personal liability coverage should equal your exposed net worth. I say "exposed" because those who have undertaken asset protection strategies that remove some of their assets from the line of fire (i.e., offshore accounts, etc.) may only need to be concerned with their U.S.-based assets. And qualified plans, as well as certain trust arrangements, may also protect a portion of their assets from liabilities.

The single purpose of personal liability coverage is to protect your assets. So, for example, if your exposed net worth is $20 million—realizing that judgments can easily reach that high—you should have at least $20 million in personal liability coverage. You also have to account for your legal expenses, which can run into seven figures. And that coverage should keep pace with the growth of your net worth.

FILLING THE GAPS

The real problem with standard umbrella policies is they are generally not designed to fill all of the major liability gaps in your primary insurance coverage. Remember Timothy and Clara? Their standard umbrella policy didn't extend to uninsured motorist coverage. If Timothy and Clara had a specialized policy that specifically added UIM coverage up to $1 million, their medical expenses would have been fully covered.

In any given family situation there could be a number of liability gaps that present significant financial exposure. Here are just a few of the more common gaps I find fairly regularly:

- *The Workers Compensation gap:* We covered this in Chapter 4, but because it is so common it's worth another mention, especially in terms of the Employers Liability Coverage, which is a part of Workers Compensation insurance. This covers your legal expenses should you be sued, and if those expenses exceed your coverage limits, you could have an expensive gap in coverage.
- *The speedboat rental gap:* In Chapter 7, we go into detail about the specific types of insurance to cover your "toys." But, what happens when you rent a speedboat or a snowmobile while away on vacation? Of course you know when you sign a rental contract you're liable for all damages and injuries while you are in possession of the toy. However, you may not be aware of the length or horsepower limitations in your homeowners coverage. If your boat is too long or too powerful, you may not be covered. If you rent toys occasionally, you should ensure your personal umbrella policy includes specific parameters to cover your particular preferences.
- *The car rental gap:* When you rent a car in the United States or Canada, your personal auto insurance typically covers the primary risk of property damage or bodily injuries whether or not you are at fault. And the secondary risk of damage to the rental may be covered depending on the type of comprehensive and collision coverage you have. Regardless, high net worth drivers shouldn't even consider renting a car unless they have separate personal liability coverage. And, if you rent a car outside of the United States or Canada, your auto policy may not cover you if you have a claim filed against you in another country. You should never rent a car outside of the United States or Canada without true "worldwide" coverage in a personal umbrella policy.

■ *The company car gap:* When driving a company car, you are generally covered under your employer's auto insurance policy. The problem arises when you are transporting a co-worker. While it's true that, if your co-worker is injured in an accident, your company's Workers Compensation insurance will cover his medical bills and lost wages, it's also true that he or she could turn around and sue you. In most cases your personal auto insurance coverage won't protect you in this situation. Your personal umbrella policy should include specific risk protection while driving the company car.

Gaps in coverage can occur wherever there is an expectation that your primary insurance, or even a standard personal umbrella policy, should provide protection, especially as your net worth and lifestyle expand. Nothing short of a comprehensive assessment of your risks can reveal the potential financial exposure these gaps present, and, if found, nothing less than a specialized personal umbrella policy will cover all contingencies.

NOT-FOR-PROFIT BOARD MEMBERS—ARE YOU AT RISK?

I am privileged to work with many high net worth clients who give so much of themselves, both in time and money, to charitable causes. By my last count, at least a third of them serve on the board of at least one and in some cases multiple nonprofit organizations. I have had a conversation with each one of them about their personal exposure while they serve on a board or even as a volunteer. Most were surprised to learn that 90 percent of claims reported by nonprofit organizations centered on injuries sustained in car accidents or onsite slip-and-falls at events sponsored by the organization.[8] But they were heartened to learn that their personal umbrella policies extended protection to board liability in at least four areas: personal injury, bodily injury, property damage, and legal defense.

But when the conversation turned to the remaining 10 percent of claims that involved allegations of improper employment practices, professional errors and omissions, financial mismanagement, and sexual harassment, they were again surprised, but equally concerned. Although these claims are far less frequent than the standard injury claim, they can be far more expensive. In fact, they account for more than 35 percent of claim dollars paid by insurers.

I always recommend that my clients obtain a copy of the organization's Employment Practices Liability, and Directors and Officers (D&O) insurance policy declaration so we can review it to ensure it has adequate coverage for occurrences not covered by their personal umbrella policy. If it does not, I recommend that they purchase a Nonprofit Directors and Officers Insurance (D&O) add-on to their personal liability policy. But here's the rub: With most policies, the add-on only provides coverage in excess of $1 million of the primary coverage required for the nonprofit's D&O policy. It's not uncommon for 501(c)3 organizations to buy less than the required amount, leaving a gap in the coverage. At least, board members need to be aware of the gap in coverage, and at most they should encourage the organization to spend the few extra bucks to bring their coverage to the required limit.

SUMMARY

Those who seek to get their "fair share" from the wealthy will not settle for less when they know what is available; so the wealthy certainly should not settle for less when it comes to protecting their assets, especially when the maximum available personal liability coverage comes at a minuscule cost.

The bigger your success and lifestyle become, the bigger your personal liability becomes. I've talked about the financial exposure of bigger homes and more expensive cars. But, as I cover in the next few chapters, every new toy, every step up in lifestyle, and each additional rung up the ladder of wealth and public visibility adds more liabilities. Having the right umbrella policy is but one, albeit critical, step in the overall risk management strategy the wealthy must undertake in order to protect their families and their assets.

CHAPTER 7

Toys, Toys, and More Toys

Sitting down for coffee with Michael, a client who's contemplating the purchase of a $2.8 million yacht, I started in on the age-old "money can't/can buy happiness" theme. As a rule, I wouldn't raise the issue with my wealthy clients for fear of striking a sensitive chord, but this client is my close skiing buddy, and he is always happy to share his insights on how the wealthy think. Without hesitation he told me that he couldn't be certain of it unless he had ample opportunity to test the theory himself. "Sure, money can buy happiness, but happiness is fleeting." He went on after a sip of coffee, "What it can't buy is contentment, which is what we all want; but for people who have the energy and resources, it's ever-elusive." He then added this clarification: "Ben Franklin was once asked what his definition of a wealthy man was, and he said, 'He who is contented.' When asked who that is, he said, 'Nobody.'" For Michael, his contentment will not come from his pursuit of money, rather from his pursuit of his passion, which is sailing.

He happily admitted that the yacht is an expression of his status and his success. He is an avid sailor and has been for most of his life. He has owned the whole gamut of boats—from an 18-foot Sea Ray to a 36-foot sailboat—all of which have brought him great joy. But just as he has never been content with his level of success in business—which is why, he says, he will never stop working—he has never been content in the pursuit of his passion. Does that mean he will eventually graduate to a 100-foot yacht? He couldn't answer that because he doesn't know how far his new 76-foot yacht will take him in his pursuit.

As Michael explained, he really hasn't changed much as a person in the short time he has been "wealthy." As to the toys he buys today, he says he is no different from others who are intent on pursuing their passion; it's just that his toys are bigger and more expensive. He was happy when he had a 12-foot sailboat, but he wasn't content, which is why he saved his money to buy an 18-foot sailboat, and so on. That's what impassioned people do. And, if one has the financial ability to continue to pursue contentment, then, why not? I did get him to admit that at least a part of his discontentment stems from the need to "keep up with the Jones." "Of course," he said with wry smile, "but at least I won't go broke while trying."

That seemed like the perfect segue into the real reason for our getting together. Michael wanted to talk about his risk exposures with his bigger and more expensive yacht, and what he needed to do to protect himself. As a longtime client, Michael understands that all of the wealth in the world can't prevent mistakes and tragic mishaps. No one is infallible.

But the problem with bigger and more expensive toys is that they tend to multiply the odds of misfortune, as well as the risk exposure. Yachts in particular are essentially floating luxury dwellings. They often carry smaller watercraft and are crewed by employees, each of which carries its own exposures. And, while Michael is wealthy enough that a complete loss of his yacht wouldn't necessarily hurt him financially, it's the tens of millions of dollars in additional liability that worries him.

CASE-IN-POINT

When they're not cruising from one exotic port to another, yachts are moored social venues where their owners entertain for business, pleasure, and status purposes. While yacht owners, as party hosts, are subject to the same liability issues as if a social function were held in their home, the fact that the venue is floating on water raises the stakes significantly.

Just last year, a high-profile yacht owner was entertaining a group of people when one of his friends became heavily intoxicated and slipped and fell into the water as he tried to step off the gangplank. As he fell toward the water, he hit his head on the gangplank and was knocked unconscious. The owner, along with several other friends, jumped in to retrieve him, but he was unresponsive when they pulled him from the water. He was pronounced dead on arrival at the hospital; the cause was attributed to drowning.

It was determined that the man had cocaine in his system and that his blood-alcohol level was more than double the legal limit. The family filed a $20 million wrongful death lawsuit claiming that the gangplank connecting the boat to the dock was "inherently dangerous," because one side of the railing was missing. Of course, it is the boat owner's responsibility to make sure the railing is fully secure.

Had the intoxicated friend slipped and hit his head in the owner's home, it is likely the liability would have been limited to injury damages, which can be an expensive claim but nowhere near the size of a wrongful death claim. A home floating on water multiplies the odds of misfortune and the risk exposure.

MANAGING YOUR RISKS AT SEA . . .

Risk management for pleasure craft is becoming more specialized and complex. Lifelong boaters who reach the next level will find that operating a yacht is a little more involved than just boats and motors. Suddenly, they are faced with myriad new expenses, regulations, and risks that significantly raise the stakes. People who can afford to buy yachts can be expected to also afford the annual expense of maintaining them; however, few are fully prepared for the onslaught of new regulations and insurance requirements that come with yacht ownership.

For many new yacht owners, the most complex new risk they need to manage is a paid crew. Unlike hiring of a household staff, which is guided by general liability and employment laws, hiring, maintaining, and protecting a yacht crew falls within the purview of myriad laws, such as the Jones Act, general maritime law, the Death on the High Seas Act, and the Federal Longshore and Harbor Workers Compensation Act.

When constructing insurance coverage for your yacht, the liability coverage needs to be tightly aligned with the requirements of these laws. At a minimum, a yacht policy needs to coordinate the amount of liability that is carried with the number of crew listed on the declarations page. And yacht owners should not rely on their personal umbrella policies to cover their crew, especially since the cost of increasing liability under a yacht policy is minimal.

Covering the Crew

Crew coverage is especially critical to protect against liabilities that arise out of their behavior that result in the death or injury of anyone on board your yacht. It is a well-established principle of maritime law that a ship owner and, by extension, the crew owe a duty of exercising reasonable care toward those lawfully aboard the vessel.

In an actual case, a yacht owner asked a crew member to take some guests to shore in a tender. The crew member had been drinking, and when the tender approached the dock, he failed to slow in time before it rammed another boat, killing one guest and severely injuring the other two. The settlement reached $15 million.

Paid crews are a whole new ballgame for new yacht owners, who require a full understanding of the owner's legal responsibilities while docked or at sea. Nothing short of a specialized insurance carrier experienced in maritime coverage can provide the level of risk management needed to fully protect yacht owners, but yacht owners should also review their personal umbrella policies as to whether they address coverage for their crew.

Navigation Exclusions and Restrictions

One of the reasons why the wealthy buy yachts is for their ability to take them on extended excursions to exotic locations. What some new yacht owners may not realize is that their insurance carriers may have something to say about their destinations. Most yacht policies include navigation limits, exclusions, and restrictions.

For example, a carrier might have a north–south warranty that requires your yacht to remain north of a specific latitude on the east coast during hurricane season. Or a policy may include a navigation exclusion that restricts transit around the coastal waters of Cuba and certain central or South American countries. If you have an experienced captain and crew, a good insurance broker will be able to work with you to develop itineraries or storm plans that might pass muster with your insurance carrier's underwriters, who can then grant you navigation extensions.

Key Features of Yacht Coverage

Yacht policies provided through specialized maritime insurers should include the following coverage at a minimum:

- *Agreed value coverage:* Pays the entire agreed amount for a total loss less your deductible.
- *Replacement cost loss settlement:* Pays for the repair or replacement of covered property for partial losses with no deduction for depreciation.
- *Liability protection:* Provides customized limits of coverage for legal costs, Jones Act coverage for paid crew, pollution cleanup, and wreck removal.
- *Medical payments:* Pays the reasonable medical costs on a per-person basis for anyone injured onboard or while boarding or leaving the yacht.
- *Uninsured boater coverage:* Pays medical costs for anyone on your yacht who is injured by an uninsured owner of another watercraft.
- *Oil Pollution Act of 1990 (OPA) coverage:* Provides for up to $10,000 of coverage for fines incurred as a result of environmental damage.
- *Longshore and Harbor Workers Compensation Act (LHWCA) coverage:* Provides coverage for workers not covered under the Jones Act.

Additional recommended coverage includes:

- Personal property and fishing equipment coverage
- Search and rescue/emergency services
- Towing and assistance

- Tender/dinghy coverage
- Trailer coverage
- Boat show and demonstration coverage
- Automatic coverage for marinas as Additional Insured
- Hurricane haul-out coverage

As with most other forms of insurance, the deductibles on a yacht policy can have a significant impact on the premium as well as the level of coverage provided. The major deductible that is applied is for hull coverage and can range from 0 percent (in no-fault cases) to as much as .25 percent of hull value. Some carriers will reduce the deductible for a period of time if you are loss free. Other deductibles can be applied to personal property and fishing equipment. As with any other type of deductible, you can exchange higher deductibles for higher liability limits and lower premiums.

Watch Out for Exclusions

Carriers will differ in their use of exclusions, so it is important to pay attention to the language in your policy. Ideally, a yacht policy should be an all-risk policy that covers all perils with minimal named exclusions. Additionally, your policy shouldn't include an exclusion for manufacturer's defects.

Depreciation in Partial Losses

Another provision that varies greatly from carrier to carrier is the depreciation terms in the policy for payment of partial losses. The issue is whether the policy will replace older engine parts with new parts or pay only the depreciated value. This applies to any property or fishing equipment that is lost or damaged. High-end policies will not depreciate inboard engines or personal property.

Working with a Marine Insurance Specialist

More than most types of insurance coverage, designing the optimum yacht policy requires a true collaboration between you and an experienced marine insurance specialist. You are responsible for keeping all of your documents up to date, such as storm plans, itineraries, captain and crew resumes, surveys, and closing statements; and your broker is responsible for constantly seeking the best policy coverage for any new or specific risk at a competitive price. Any changes to your documentation that are not communicated to your broker could result in the declination of coverage.

. . . AND IN THE AIR

Flying is another passion pursued by the wealthy, but it is also deemed as a more practical mode of transportation by business executives and entrepreneurs who don't want to deal with the incontinences of public air travel. In either case, people who buy airplanes or jets are certainly aware of the ultimate risk involved. The issue is whether they have taken the proper measures to fully protect themselves and their families against all possible risks.

The good news/bad news about airplane accidents is that they don't occur as frequently as other types of transportation accidents; but when they do occur, they are usually devastating to people and property. The other good news, if you want to call it that, is that most airplane accidents occur while the aircraft is parked at gate, taxing for takeoff, or returning to the gate. Somewhere in between are the accidents that occur during takeoff or landing—some can be disastrous, but most people survive these mishaps. But aircraft owners need to sweat the small stuff as much as they sweat the big stuff.

Another Case-in-Point

An owner-pilot took a colleague along on a short business trip in his plane and, upon their return, the landing gear did not retract completely, resulting in a hard landing that injured the passenger. His medical costs were only $80,000, but he decided to sue his pilot-colleague for $1 million.

Key Components of Aviation Coverage

Aviation insurance has some unique characteristics. Aircraft liability limits are covered on an occurrence basis and very large liability limits are readily available; and there are no aggregate limits applied with the exception of product liability and personal injury liability. Aviation policies are extremely broad and usually include coverage for flood or earthquake. The policies are considered "all risk" but are subject to some very important exclusions and limitations that you need to understand. These exclusions and limitations vary from one insurance company to the next so it is important to understand these terms and read the coverage offers carefully. At a minimum, an aviation insurance policy should include these key components:

Third-Party Liability Coverage and Liability Limits   As with automobile coverage, aviation insurance comes with specific liability limits that are defined on the coverage summary page of the policy. Liability coverage is broken down into Bodily Injury (BI) and Property Damage (PD), and, in most policy forms, both limits are written as a Combined Single Limit (CSL) as opposed to stating them as separate liability limits. Some policies include *smooth limit liability*, which includes passenger bodily injury in their CSL, while others cover passengers through an endorsement. Policies that split out passenger liability coverage tend to restrict liability to a *per-passenger-seat* or *per-passenger* claim. For instance, if your CSL is $1 million, your per-passenger liability may be limited to $100,000 per passenger.

Generally, liability limits are established by insurers based on pilot experience, the type of aircraft, and purpose of use. In recent years, insurers have been raising liability limits to as high as $10 million on a CSL smooth limit liability basis. As with other types of insurance, liability coverage for aircraft can be relatively inexpensive. Without proper third-party liability coverage, you leave open the possibility of having to pay all or a part of the claim out of your own pocket.

But wait—won't my umbrella policy provide additional liability coverage for me and my aircraft? It's vitally important to note that personal umbrella policies rarely extend coverage to aviation exposures. Read through your personal umbrella and chances are you will find an exclusion for aviation exposures. Not all umbrella policies have this exclusion as the umbrella liability policy wording does vary from one company to the next. Should your umbrella policy provide coverage for aviation, you then need to look at who owns the aircraft. Many aircraft are owned by corporations or LLCs, which are viewed as separate legal entities. Your umbrella policy, if it provides aircraft coverage, may require the aircraft to be owned in your personal name. This is an area often misunderstood and/or overlooked. Before you fly, know how your umbrella policy handles your aviation exposure.

Hull Coverage   As with a boat, the hull of the aircraft is comprised of the body and all permanently attached equipment and modifications. Hull coverage is placed on an *agreed value* basis, which is the amount you and your underwriter agree the aircraft is worth. The amount stated as the agreed value at the time of policy issuance is the amount paid in the event of a total loss and the loss payment is not reduced by depreciation—pretty straightforward.

In aircraft insurance parlance, a *total loss* is the result of the disappearance or theft of the entire aircraft, or when the cost to repair physical damage exceeds the insured value. Historically, insurers were willing to deem aircraft 70 percent damaged as a total loss because they could recoup a fair amount through salvage—it would be cheaper to simply replace the aircraft than to repair it. More recently, as aircraft values have declined, reducing their salvage value, insurers have been more reluctant to declare a 70 percent damaged aircraft a total loss because it can be cheaper to repair the aircraft, especially if the aircraft is overinsured.

Where aircraft owners often run into trouble is in arriving at an agreed value that doesn't expose them to either overinsurance or underinsurance. Inherent in the agreed-value contract is the danger of overinsuring your aircraft. Aircraft values have been declining over the last several years, which has led to aircraft being insured for more than their market value. If a partially destroyed aircraft has more hull coverage than its market value, the insurer will have to consider whether it is a total loss, which should be completely replaced, or whether it would be less expensive to repair. The latter outcome would leave you with a repaired aircraft that would not attract a lot of flying buddies, not to mention prospective buyers.

It is vitally important to have your aircraft appraised frequently with appropriate adjustments made to your coverage. If you are not comfortable with the stated value in your policy, it can be changed through an endorsement or upon policy renewal. It's always advisable to work with an experienced aviation insurance specialist in determining the appropriate value for your aircraft.

Medical Coverage Medical coverage pays for minor medical costs regardless of who is at fault. The standard medical coverage will pay up to $1,000 per occupant, although coverage can be purchased up to $3,000. In most policies medical coverage is optional, which is why it is sometimes overlooked. Medical coverage is recommended largely because it will prevent having to file a claim against your bodily injury liability coverage.

Deductibles Deductibles play a big part in determining the cost of coverage. As with other types of insurance, the deductible is the amount of money that the insured has at risk and is paid toward the loss before the insurer pays the claim. Typically, aircraft insurance includes two types of deductibles: one for *in-motion* (IM) losses and one for *in-flight* (IF) losses. IM losses occur when the aircraft's engines are running, enabling the aircraft to move on its own power. So, that could be sitting on the tarmac or taxiing. IF losses occur between the time the aircraft begins its takeoff roll and it comes to a stop after landing.

Other deductibles may apply, depending on the type of aircraft. For instance, water-alighting aircraft may have an in-mooring deductible and turbine-powered aircraft coverage may have an ingestion deductible. You could also see policies that impose separate deductibles for gear collapse or windstorm damage.

Exclusions What would an insurance policy be without exclusions? How about much easier to understand? While that may be true, exclusions serve to clarify, and sometimes it's easier to know a policy by what it doesn't cover than what it does cover. We know, for example, that exclusions are those losses that are not insurable under any circumstances. They may also be expressed as coverage that is available but only at an additional premium charge because it is an additional risk. You pay the extra premium and the risk is covered. Or, they could be losses that would be or should be covered by another policy.

The good news is that many of the exclusions are fairly straightforward, but as with any insurance policy they need to be fully understood in their context, and aircraft coverage can be somewhat more complex.

Among some of the exclusions applicable to aircraft coverage are:

- *Pilot and use:* Coverage is not available when the aircraft is being operated by non-approved pilots and/or is being used in a way not allowed in the policy.
- *Bodily injury to the pilot:* Liability coverage extends only to other people injured, not to the pilot, who is generally covered by his or her own medical insurance.
- *Bodily injury to employees of the pilot:* Passengers injured while flying in their capacity as an employee for you or the company are generally covered under Workers Compensation plans.
- *Territorial limitations:* The geographical limits stated in the policy in which your aircraft is covered. Standard aviation policies generally limit the territory of operation to the 48 contiguous states and some parts of Canada and Mexico. Other policies might extend the limits to the Western Hemisphere while there are also some that allow operation anywhere in the world. This is a critical exclusion to fully understand because if you incur a liability outside of the stated territorial limits, your coverage will be declined.

Aircraft coverage also contains many of the standard exclusions found in other types of insurance; however, there are a few twists that pertain to aircraft owners.

- *Wear and tear:* Losses caused by mechanical breakdown or electrical failure, deterioration, or freezing are excluded. Parts that are designed to wear out, such as brakes and tires, are also not covered. However, any losses arising from *downstream damage* may be covered under certain conditions. For example, if as a result of a mechanical failure your aircraft begins to lose oil pressure, causing engine parts to break free and fly through the cowling and into the wing, the breaking of engine parts is not covered by the policy; however, the downstream damage of the shattered cowling and damaged wing is covered.

■ *War exclusions:* War exclusions have been a staple of most types of insurance for decades and aircraft insurance has been no exception, until fairly recently. The typical war exclusion wrapped several forms of "man-caused" disasters, such as war, martial law, a coup, atomic blasts, strikes, riots, terrorist acts, sabotage, and hijacking, into one broad exclusion. Since the terrorist attacks of 2001, and the general heating up of global strife, aircraft owners are much more inclined to add this coverage, which can now be done through an endorsement for an additional premium.

Who Owns the Aircraft?

One of the more critical factors is ownership. Flying enthusiasts tend to register their aircraft in their name, while company owners and executives are likely to purchase it as "corporate aircraft." In the latter case, the aircraft is typically flown by professional pilots for the purpose of transporting the owner or the owner's employees and guests on personal and business trips, thus multiplying the odds of misfortune and risk exposure.

Limited liability companies (LLCs) are a common form of aircraft ownership. The LLC is made up of members; sometimes these are individuals but corporations can also be members. As part of personal risk management it is important to keep the LLC agreement up-to-date and documented to take into account unforeseen circumstances of the LLC's members. The unforeseen circumstances can include the member who gets a divorce. Perhaps a member falls on difficult financial times and can no longer afford his financial share of the aircraft. The corporation that is a member of the LLC may go bankrupt. Circumstances like these need to be reviewed and documented before you take flight.

There are additional issues associated with the ownership and operation of corporate aircraft that tend to be larger and more complex than for leisure aircraft. Pilots need to be recruited, screened, and hired. It requires a staffed maintenance facility in order to stay on top of the myriad maintenance issues and the all-critical maintenance recordkeeping requirements. Hangars have to be built, and office space must be available for personnel involved with all aspects of maintaining the aircraft.

Whether the aircraft is owned individually or by a corporation is a factor in determining who the responsible parties are, which can be somewhat convoluted. For instance, you may own your aircraft but fly it occasionally for business purposes. In this case, both you and your company can be listed as responsible parties providing third parties with a much deeper pocket. A corporate jet owner might carry as much as $20 million of liability coverage per passenger seat. But individual aircraft owners may not see the need for such high limits.

Using an individual aircraft for both business and pleasure multiplies the odds of misfortune as well as the risk exposure. It all comes down to the "Purpose of Use" provision in the policy that states the allowable uses for the aircraft. There is a big difference in coverage among the many different uses, such as pleasure, business, commercial, charter, instruction, and cargo hauling. Flying an aircraft outside the stated purpose of use could result in a declination of coverage.

Who's Flying the Aircraft?

Many aircraft owners, especially corporate owners, hire a flight crew, some full-time and others on an as-needed basis. In all cases, pilot operators need to be approved under the aircraft owner's insurance policy. This requires that pilots must meet the minimum requirements as stated in the policy through an open pilot warranty, or by being specifically named as an approved pilot. If a pilot is not approved under the policy, the aircraft owner could face a declination of coverage. It should be noted that the FAA has its own requirements for non-owner pilots; however, they tend to be less restrictive than the aviation insurance underwriters' requirements.

Aircraft owners must be clear on the distinction between *approved* pilots and *insured* pilots. The owner's insurance coverage does not necessarily extend to the approved pilot. Approved pilots need to carry their own insurance protection if it is not extended to them by the owner's policy.

Don't Forget Non-Owned Auto Insurance

Yes, we are talking about aircraft; however, how do you expect to get around at those destinations where you need to conduct business or drive into town for a meal? Aircraft owners who use the services of *fixed-based operators* (FBO) can sometimes arrange for loaner cars to tool around in while their aircraft is being serviced or housed. Sometimes cars are loaned if available, and other FBOs will offer to rent a car. In either case, the driver of the car still may be required to show proof of insurance if he or she is visiting out-of-state. However, many business auto insurance policies don't include liability coverage for non-owned autos unless it is added as an endorsement. For a few dollars a month, this additional coverage can provide the extra layer of protection that can make your trip that much more secure.

Working with an Aviation Insurance Specialist

As you can see, there are a lot of moving parts in aviation coverage. An insurance broker with at least minimal knowledge and connections with aviation insurance should be able to obtain a minimal level of coverage. But, that's where the basics of aviation coverage end, and the need for expert aviation risk management begins. There are just too many variables and factors that need to be thoroughly considered in order to ensure the optimum level of coverage. Anyone who is not an expert in aviation coverage couldn't possibly address them all, let alone the most critical factors. The outcome could be financially devastating for the aircraft owner.

Unlike other types of property and casualty insurance, aviation insurance has not been reduced to a commodity. While it is a highly specialized market, the fierce competition among the relatively few carriers coupled with lower margins creates a more fluid and somewhat unpredictable environment for underwriting aviation insurance. While every insurer shares the same goal of making an underwriting profit, they don't share their data, trends, claims, or rate information with one another, so there is no consistency in premium rates. Also, the different insurers have different appetites in each of the class risks, so you never know what you're going to get.

That's why it is vitally important that you work with an experienced aviation insurance specialist, one who is not only intimately familiar with the market, but who can also navigate the critical application submission process. The quality of the submission by the broker is the only thing the underwriter has to determine the quality of the risk presented, and that entails an accurate and full description of the risk as well as the organization of the submission itself.

YOU'D BETTER SWEAT THE SMALL STUFF

With all of this talk about yachts and airplanes, it would be easy to relegate any discussion of the smaller toys to an afterthought, but that would be a huge mistake. First, there are many more high net worth families that own the smaller recreational vehicles, such as all-terrain vehicles, snowmobiles, and jet-skis, than there are those who own yachts and aircraft. Second, small, high-powered recreational vehicles present no less risk exposure than a large pleasure boat.

In fact, the risk of injury or death with a jet-ski or snowmobile is far greater than with an airplane. An injury or death caused by an ATV accident is no less costly than one caused by a capsized yacht. And, many wealthy families can't just own one or two; they often own a garage-full in each of their homes. So, when you multiply the number of toys you own, you also multiply the odds of misfortune as well as your risk exposure.

The Homeowners Insurance Fallacy

While it is true that your homeowners insurance offers certain types of coverage for your ATV and snowmobile, it is limited and only provides coverage when they are operated on your home site. And you will also find specific limitations or exclusions in the liability coverage of your homeowners policy. Jet-skis are considered to be watercraft and typically excluded from liability and medical payments coverage. While conditions, restrictions, and exclusions may vary slightly from one homeowners policy to the next, it can be generally concluded that the only way to ensure maximum protection against bodily injury claims is with individual liability coverage for each type of craft.

ATV Coverage

It is commonly and mistakenly thought that ATVs, because they don't need to be registered, are not excluded from coverage in a homeowners policy. While that may be true, the coverage is limited to homestead use, so, if it is used off-road and off the homestead, as is often the case, there is no coverage. Without question, however, your homeowners liability coverage will not follow you off-road and away from your home. Liability protection for you and anyone who operates the vehicle, needs to be your greatest concern.

Although separate ATV insurance is not mandatory (except in some state parks), it is highly advisable, especially for high net worth individuals. ATV insurance works much the same as auto or motorcycle insurance and it protects you both on road and off. You can buy both damage protection and liability coverage, but you can keep your premiums low by skipping the damage protection and maxing out on the liability coverage.

Snowmobile Coverage

It is well-documented that a powerful engine on ice and snow is a deadly combination. Because of the high accident rate, many insurers are becoming much more risk adverse with snowmobile coverage often requiring special training certification, and boosting premiums on some of the more powerful models.

As with ATVs, a homeowners policy provides limited coverage for snowmobiles operated on your property. Once off the property, they are not covered. In many states and in Canada, snowmobile insurance is mandatory, so, if your vacation plans take you there, you need to have it. With most policies, the coverage will follow you to any state.

Jet-Skis (Personal Watercraft—PWC)

Jet-skis are considered to be watercraft, the same as any engine-powered boat, so they fall within the purview of maritime and admiralty laws. They are also like very powerful motorcycles on water, exposing the operator and riders to immense risks. Both damage and liability coverage for PWC are typically excluded from homeowners policies, and while it's not mandatory in some states, separate PWC insurance is essential for high net worth individuals.

Motor Home (RV) Coverage

A growing trend among high net worth families is to purchase or lease vacant sites at a lake or near a beach, or both, and then visit them throughout the year in their luxury motor home. It's a great alternative to purchasing and maintaining multiple vacation homes and it offers much more flexibility in planning vacations. It also is much easier to manage from a risk exposure standpoint. Motor home policies cover liabilities arising from injuries or damage whether it is being driven or parked. The only catch is that it doesn't cover liability when injuries or property damage occur on the site on which the motor home is parked. The solution is very simple. For $20 to $30 a year, you can add liability coverage for your site through an endorsement on your homeowners liability coverage.

CHAPTER 8

Personal and Family Security Risks

In the aftermath of the calamitous economic and fiscal events over the past several years, the high net worth community should forget about asking "Are we better off today than we were four years ago?" We should instead ponder the more salient question: "Are we safer today than we were four years ago?" The ever-widening wealth gap and income disparity in our country provides some evidence that the wealthy—or 1 percent—are better off financially, at least relative to the 99 percent who, egged on by the class warfare drumbeat of certain politicians and the media, have channeled their discontent into Main Street rage. A perfect storm of prolonged economic distress, political ineptitude, and Wall Street envy has much of the high-net-worth community fearing for the safety of their families.

Recent trends portend an undeniable increase in the threats facing the wealthy, including:

- Continued class warfare assaults on the wealthy by politicians and the media
- Increased incidences of workplace violence by disgruntled employees
- A marked increase in the number of home invasions and burglaries
- The infiltration of family offices by organized crime groups
- A sharp uptick in the number of reported extortion cases
- Greater access to private information via the web, either by hacking or by sophisticated search methods
- An increase in shareholder grievances over corporate governance
- Increased anti-American sentiment overseas
- Increasing terrorist activities at home and abroad

Wealth certainly has its privileges; however, it's not without some elements of risk. A Zogby survey conducted in 2011 reports that 92 percent of wealthy individuals lose sleep over the possibility of home invasions, muggings, and random street crime; and many haven't even considered the more likely threat of identity theft or cyberattacks.[9] Interestingly, more than half of the respondents are taking steps to shrink the target on their backs by downsizing their lifestyle. The problem in this increasingly transparent, digital world is that it is nearly impossible to fly under the radar. The good news is that advances in preemptive security and risk mitigation can substantially reduce the threat.

WHOM ARE WE REALLY DEALING WITH HERE?

Unfortunately, wealth attracts unwanted attention from unsavory characters bent on utilizing any available method to redistribute it in their favor. No, I'm not talking about politicians, although one can easily make the case to include them in that category. And, contrary to conventional wisdom, the two-bit criminal doesn't target the rich, preferring instead the low-hanging fruit of the more vulnerable, such as the elderly, the mom-and-pop shop, and just about any unsuspecting person with cash in his or her wallet. Rather, the wealthy are high-value targets for the more sophisticated criminal elements with access to technology and highly skilled specialists.

Utilizing advanced techniques once thought to be the exclusive domain of the FBI, these twenty-first-century criminals, typically backed by a U.S.-based or international crime syndicate, conduct extensive surveillance, searching the depths of cyberspace for information. They will even penetrate their mark's inner circle before launching their assault in the form of a home invasion, extortion, cyberattack, identity theft, or fraud.

Because most of the incidences of wealth crimes we hear about occur with celebrities, non-celebrities are apt to believe that it can't happen to them, because they keep a low profile. In reality, these criminals aren't particular about the entertainment value of their marks, just their bank account value. If they can dig up information on you that can be used or sold, you will become a target.

WE'RE ALL AN OPEN BOOK

As I am writing this, the newswires are reporting that the FBI is conducting a major investigation into allegations that the financial records of certain political figures were illicitly accessed. It appears that a website with the Internet domain .su, which implies a Russian-based domain, published credit reports, banking information, Social Security numbers, and home addresses of such notables as Vice President Biden, First Lady Michelle Obama, Attorney General

Eric Holder, and Hillary Clinton. Celebrities such as Kim Kardashian, Ashton Kutcher, Arnold Schwarzenegger, and Beyoncé were also victimized. The FBI is trying to determine if this is a case of identity theft, hacking, or both.

On the same day, it was reported that former Secretary of State Colin Powell's Facebook and personal e-mail accounts were hacked, and scanned images of the digital correspondence were sent to newspaper journalists. In the previous month several members of the Bush family also reported that their e-mail accounts had been breached.

To demonstrate just how vulnerable sports figures are to information hackers, CBS SportsLine.com conducted an investigation to demonstrate how easy it is to unearth the most sensitive personal information.[10] The results were stunning:

- Within minutes, the home address of a sports league commissioner was uncovered.
- The signature of a national championship basketball coach was found on a mortgage document.
- The signature of Tiger Woods was found on property deeds.
- The signatures and Social Security numbers of a high-profile college football coach and his wife were found on mortgage documents. In addition, their divorce records were also accessed.
- The signature of a well-known professional quarterback was found on a property deed.
- A legal document was found naming Mike Ditka as power of attorney. The document also listed his Social Security number.

This is only a partial list of what was uncovered, and had it not been for the investigation, none of these people would have been aware that their signatures and personal information were accessible—the same information that cyber-thieves, criminals, and fraudsters use in the commission of their crimes.

Obviously, the less public information on an individual that is out there, the lower the risk that it will be accessed. But keeping information out of the public eye is difficult in the digital age. When you buy a home, a boat, or a plane, it becomes part of the public record. Although certain records are not supposed to be accessible for public viewing, state and local agencies push mountains of information out to the Internet *cloud*, often using archaic technology that allows a lot of it to fall through the cracks. At the very least, high net worth individuals may not want to register purchases in their own name with their personal information.

Cybercriminals can look just about anywhere to dig up vital information. For example, if an aircraft owner's plane has a recognizable name, such as *Trump*, anyone can access aviation records to check destinations along with departure and arrival times. Or, if a wealthy couple donates a large sum of money to a charitable organization, it may become a part of the public record. All of this information can be used by cyber-trollers to plan a crime.

Whom Can You Trust?

Security experts point to the inner circle of the wealthy as the most likely sources of information leaks that can be used plan a criminal assault. "Trusting the wrong people" is said to be the greatest vulnerability of high-net-worth people who rely on household staff, consultants, business associates, and advisors just to get through the day. Even the most thorough background check can't uncover a disgruntled household staff member who is approached with an offer he can't refuse.

Perhaps the weakest links in the family security chain are the younger family members. The rise of social media as a gateway for children's interaction with the world presents a substantial risk for wealthy families who otherwise try to keep a low profile. By posting details of their whereabouts, activities, and plans, family members can inadvertently compromise their family's security.

Family offices and money managers are increasingly targeted by cyber-criminals who use sophisticated techniques to penetrate the powerful firewalls guarding their clients' highly sensitive information. You've probably heard of *phishing*, a common technique used by cybercriminals to fool a person into responding to an e-mail that has been faked to look like it came from a real financial institution or government agency. When high-net-worth individuals are targeted, it's appropriately called *whaling*. This technique involves sending personally addressed e-mails to family offices, money managers, and financial advisors with links that install malicious software.

A similar technique is used to mask the caller ID of a scammer and make it appear as if it is coming from a known financial institution or trusted advisor. Victims are tricked into providing personal information for purposes of "account verification." Of course, family offices and financial professionals should know that financial institutions rarely call to verify account information.

The trust issue has two sides: First, there is the need to be able to know that the people in your inner circle are trustworthy. That can only be determined by conducting thorough and frequent background checks; second, you must be able to trust that those who do have access to vital family information have taken all possible measures to lock it down.

Identity Theft

Do you know who is on the other end of that e-mail address? It might not be as apparent as you think. Can you be sure someone isn't watching every move you make on your computer? You can't see them, but they can see every keystroke. We are all under the constant threat of a cyber-assault.

The number of people who access their financial accounts online has nearly doubled in the last couple of years. So, it isn't surprising that the number of cyber-thieves and online fraudsters has also increased. They're after your money and they are relentless in pursuing any and all technological means to get it. Because their point of entry is your computer, you are really the last line of defense in preventing an assault that could rob you of your identity and your money. The first step of prevention is to know how they can get to you.

Keystroke Logging

Also known as *keylogging*, this is a method prevalent among cyber-thieves that actually records each of your keystrokes and mouse clicks. Keyloggers gain access to your computer's operating system by imbedding a virus. From that point on, it's as if you have someone looking over your shoulder the moment you log on to your computer. Every entry of sensitive account information, log-on IDs and passwords, and PINs is captured, enabling fraudsters to gain access to your financial accounts as if they were you.

Here is how to prevent keylogging theft:

- Use reliable antivirus and antimalware programs and keep them updated.
- Update your computer's operating system. Make sure you are using the most recent security patch available.
- Monitor your financial accounts regularly, looking for unusual activity.
- Never enter personal information over a public-use computer or a computer of which you have no certainty of its security.

Phishing

Even more common is a scam referred to as phishing where fraudsters attempt to elicit personal information through phony e-mail notifications or fake websites, both created to look official and legitimate. The typical ploy is to send an e-mail that might look like it originated from a bank or government agency. In it is a request for financial information or a Social Security number that's needed to verify or update your personal account. It usually includes some form of a threat that your account will be negatively affected without action on your part. You are asked to click on a link that will take you to a website where you need to enter your information. The website is a façade for fraudsters and the information you enter is now in their hands.

Here is how to prevent a phishing attack:

- Don't open e-mails from unknown senders.
- The sender address could include the name of a bank or government agency—know the difference between fake and real addresses.
- *Never* open a link in an e-mail to a business website when a request for personal information is made. Legitimate organizations never request personal information through an e-mail.
- For general fraud protection, you should change your passwords regularly, and avoid using the same passwords on all of your accounts. Never store your log-on ID or passwords where they could be found.

In addition to these protective measures, high net worth households should be covered with identity theft coverage typically available with a homeowners policy as part of the policy or as an endorsement. The cost in terms of legal expense and time to rectify a theft can be substantial, so if the policy limits are inadequate, it is recommended that you purchase a separate identity theft insurance policy.

UNDERSTANDING THE THREATS

The vast majority of crimes perpetrated against the wealthy involve identity theft and fraud committed with the help of supposedly private information collected through security breaches. However, information security breaches also lead to more serious crimes, those feared the most by wealthy families: kidnapping, extortion, and home invasions.

The Kidnapping Threat

Although it's the rarest of high-profile criminal acts, kidnapping is the most feared threat among the wealthy. What makes it all the more heinous is that it is almost always perpetrated by someone they know, or it involves someone who has intimate knowledge of their whereabouts and activities. High-profile kidnappings usually occur in locations where the victims feel the most secure, with most occurring within view of their home or office. Abductors will spend months gathering information, conducting surveillance, getting close to people in the inner circle, and sometimes even extorting information from those closest to the intended victim.

Most kidnappings are perpetrated by serious criminals who have financial backing. Although the success rate of kidnap/ransoms in the United States is extremely low, security firms and insurers are bracing for an increase in kidnapping attempts perpetrated by anyone with a grudge and an opportunity. The highly publicized attempt on David Lettermen's son was stopped in the planning stage when his painter was turned into the police by his accomplice.

As the economy continues to drive a wedge between the "haves" and the "have-nots," as it has in parts of Europe, the rate of kidnapping attempts is expected to rise. At the extreme are countries like Italy, which averages a kidnapping each day. While it is not likely to reach that level here, it's feared that acts of desperation, including kidnappings, burglaries, and extortion, will become more commonplace.

The threat of a kidnapping is far greater for the wealthy when they travel abroad. Company executives are especially ripe targets for organized crime syndicates, which operate throughout the world. The drug lords in Mexico have turned kidnapping into a lucrative side business. At a more pedestrian level, taxi drivers in Mexico and other Central and South American countries have taken to "ATM kidnappings" where they pick up someone they mark as wealthy and then deliver them to some accomplices. The victim is driven around to ATM machines and forced to withdraw money to the maximum limit. They might hold onto victims for a couple of days in order to continue withdrawing to the maximum limit.

Of course, the best course of action a wealthy family can take is prevention, and that's where a preemptive security strategy comes into play. But as thorough as any strategy could possibly be, it can't be 100 percent effective, which is why every wealthy family should have kidnap and ransom insurance (K&R). K&R is broad coverage that will reimburse ransom payments and additional costs associated with recovering the victim. It will also cover lost ransoms, business interruption, additional security costs, and any court costs, as well as medical and death expenses. And, during the course of the kidnapping, the insured will have access to security experts who are highly trained on ransoms and recoveries, to intervene in communications with the kidnappers and law enforcement.

K&R policies are issued in amounts from $1 million up to $50 million and are customized to the personal situation of the insured. At their core, they are designed to provide peace of mind to wealthy families, regardless of where they travel.

The Extortion Threat

The same kind of security breach that can lead to a kidnapping could also lead to an extortion attempt. In fact, extortion acts are much more commonplace; but, because most aren't reported, there is no way to know how many actually occur. Every now and then we get a glimpse into the seedy world of extortion when a high-profile case is leaked to the media. You might remember the case of an Emmy Award–winning producer for CBS who was sent to prison for attempting to blackmail David Letterman for $2 million. A high-profile case like that would have a difficult time escaping the media.

But, for every case of extortion that is reported, countless others are kept quiet for fear of unwanted and embarrassing publicity. Most victims just want to pay the money in order to make the problem go away. While it's difficult to determine if extortion cases are on the rise, security firms are reporting a significant uptick in cases since 2008, a trend they attribute to the declining economy.

It used to be that the risk of extortion increased for high-profile people who are constantly in the news, because that's where perpetrators gather their information. In the highly transparent digital world, information, including that which is not meant for public viewing, is accessible to anyone who has the technical means to access it. But the biggest vulnerability for the wealthy is their inner circle, which might include business associates, household staff, or even disgruntled family members, any of whom might be willing to give up sensitive information in return for a piece of the action. Or they may be the target of extortionists themselves, threatened with a scandalous revelation if they don't provide some information on their ultimate target.

By the way, K&R insurance will also cover extortion payments and recovery costs.

THE WORLD IS YOUR LIABILITY

World travel, whether for business or pleasure, is a hallmark of the next level that presents a host of risk exposures. Liabilities and risks that most people can cover with a typical homeowners policy or travel benefits from American Express are multiplied when traveling the globe. Everything from personal liabilities to auto coverage to medical coverage suddenly becomes more complicated and traditional insurance solutions fall well short of providing the needed protection, if they provide any at all.

Driving Internationally

Driving a car in a foreign country is difficult enough when you aren't familiar with the geography, but it can be a nightmare if you don't have the right kind of insurance coverage. Relying on the pay-as-you-go coverage provided by car rental companies or other local insurers can be a costly mistake if it doesn't provide the liability limits you might need.

If you travel extensively overseas, it is imperative that you have automobile insurance that provides maximum coverage for the vehicles you drive anywhere in the world. Most luxury car insurance plans include this kind of coverage in their policy. You should also check your personal umbrella policy to ensure that it covers you worldwide.

Medical Coverage

With most health insurance plans, your full coverage stops at the shores of the United States. The good news is that most developed countries will provide medical care should you need it. The bad news is that you could be lying on a gurney for days waiting for treatment. And, if you're traveling in a third-world country, you might stand a better chance of survival by refusing treatment.

In all seriousness, if you are a frequent global traveller, you multiply the risk of becoming ill or injured overseas. The only type of medical coverage that can ensure quick and high-quality medical care is an extended travel insurance policy that provides excess medical coverage for co-pays, deductibles, and hospital charges that are not likely to be covered by your personal health insurance plan. Comprehensive travel insurance plans will also cover the expense of emergency transportation to quality medical facilities.

Personal and Family Security Abroad

Personal security risks were covered extensively in the previous section, but the emphasis here is on the safety and security of yourself and your family while traveling abroad. It is an unfortunate sign of the times that crisis-events, such as kidnappings and extortion, are becoming more prevalent, targeting the rich wherever they might go. While much rarer (or at least much less publicized) here in the United States, these threats are on the increase in countries with troubled economies like Greece and Italy. But, they've always been a risk in countries throughout Europe, South America, and Asia.

Anyone with wealth is a target for crime syndicates that prey on the unprepared. Nothing short of a comprehensive insurance package that includes access to security consultants can provide the essential protection. This would include kidnap-for-ransom and extortion insurance as well as training in the basic principles of security. It can also include immediate response to any crisis-event anywhere in the world. Specialty insurers such as AIG offer comprehensive personal security plans with the expertise to implement protective measures that will substantially reduce the threat.

PREEMPTIVE SECURITY PLANNING

It is a very sad sign of our times that the wealthy have become the object of scorn among those who don't realize or choose to ignore how much they contribute to society and the economy. A case can be made that some people border on the unscrupulous in their pursuit of wealth at the expense of others. But most people who achieve success and wealth are highly sensitive to the responsibilities they bring and give freely of their money and time to help people who are less fortunate. Unfortunately, cybercriminals, fraudsters, extortionists, kidnappers, and opportunists don't differentiate between the "bad" wealthy and the "good" wealthy.

The vulnerable in the high net worth community are the newly wealthy, those who have just arrived at the next level and who have yet to fully comprehend their additional security exposure. While many of these people may find comfort behind the guarded gates of a posh community in the confines of a home tricked out with a state-of-the-art security system, they sometimes can't begin to know how vulnerable they really are until they are attacked. Unfortunately, most preemptive planning and countermeasure strategies aren't put in place until after a threat occurs. However, better late than never, because threats are always present.

Home Security Systems

I mentioned state-of-the-art home security systems and alluded to the notion that they are not the cure-all. Unquestionably, there are some real space-age systems out there, replete with the ability to detect minute changes in airflow, sound waves, temperature, and even weight. Hidden cameras keep an eye on household staff, and perimeter systems keep intruders at bay. They come with voice, face, or retinal recognition, and they can be operated and monitored from a smartphone anywhere in the world. They are truly amazing, that is, if you actually use them the way they are designed to be used. Several of my clients have invested huge sums into these systems only to find that they can be very inconvenient because they are too complex to operate, or too disruptive to their day-to-day activities.

Home security systems are essential because they are the last line of defense; but to be effective, they have to be practical. Throwing money at bells and whistles will not improve security if they are not versed in the habits and lifestyle of the family. The recommended course families should take is to work with a risk management firm's security experts to design a system around their needs, concerns, and lifestyle. It's important to achieve a balance between overzealous security and being able to freely live a good life. To that end, a practical, usable home security system is only a starting point for the countermeasures a wealthy family must have in place. A preemptive security plan involves many layers beyond wires and alarms.

Plugging the Security Leaks

In addition to increasing home security, wealthy families should have a complete security apparatus as part of a controlled and coordinated risk management strategy. At a minimum, the following countermeasures should be considered as essential components:

- *Identity theft protection:* This includes 24/7 monitoring of credit bureaus and financial accounts, along with cyber-security measures to prevent hacking and malicious attacks on computers. Special attention needs to be given to guard against the loss of wallets, and sensitive documents that aren't securely stored should be shredded daily. Mail should be delivered to a secure location.
- *Systematic background investigations:* These should be conducted by highly trained specialists upon initial screening and hiring and at least once per year. In addition to investigating work history, criminal history, credit history, and education credentials, these investigations should include a deep assessment of character and integrity ascertained through interviews of past employers, family members, and associates of the prospective employee.
- *Cyber-security:* This should include a formal information security policy to be implemented among all family members and staff. A complete assessment of network vulnerability should be conducted and appropriate cyber-protection equipment installed and monitored.
- *Global travel intelligence:* This involves assessing the threat of kidnapping and other risks involved in travel to any destination. Itineraries are developed around "safe" hotels, airports, and travel routes.

Education as the Most Effective Countermeasure

The personal risk footprint of wealthy families can stretch far beyond their homes. It follows them wherever they go, sometimes rendering the most sophisticated equipment and countermeasure strategies ineffective. That's why the most effective countermeasure strategy is education, that is, having a full understanding of all threats, how they can materialize, and how to avoid them. It need not be as draconian as it sounds, as if you have to go through life constantly looking over your shoulder. It's more about having an awareness of your surroundings, your actions, and the company you keep.

Working with a qualified risk management and security specialist to implement a coordinated, preemptive strategy, you should be able to live a perfectly normal life. But we all have to take some responsibility for our personal safety by understanding the threats.

CHAPTER 9

The Dangers of Wealth

Having achieved remarkable success at a young age, Robert was already looking for other challenges. At age 39, he had built his small auto parts store into a regional chain with 40 stores and he eventually sold it to a larger chain. With a net worth of more than $25 million, he would never have to work again. Politics always interested him, and being as active as he was in the community and charity organizations, he was constantly being recruited by political organizations to run for office. He decided to run for an open political seat, so he set out on the luncheon circuit to build support among the community elite.

During the course of a question-and-answer session at one luncheon, Robert was asked what he thought of a particular opponent who had a reputation for being a womanizer. Being a political novice, Robert didn't sidestep the question as he should have; instead he made a comment about a "revolving door of women at his [opponent's] house." While he did get a laugh out of the audience, little did he know that a women sitting in the back of the room was Twittering his comment to the entire world. It was re-tweeted more than 10,000 times within the next few hours and it made the front page of the local paper.

Although Robert apologized publicly for his comments, his opponent threatened him with a defamation lawsuit, more for political purposes than anything else. Fortunately for Robert, his opponent was nearly as wealthy as he was, and he really didn't want his dirty laundry aired in the media and the courts, so he didn't pursue it. Robert went on to win the election, but he learned a very important lesson the hard way.

HIGH PROFILE EQUALS HIGH RISK

Robert, who is now my client, was always aware that his wealth created more risk exposure for him, but this episode made him acutely aware that his status as a public figure multiplied his risk odds substantially. Even if he hadn't decided to run for public office, as a high-profile CEO of a successful company, he is a de facto celebrity. Not only are his activities of interest to the media and the general public, but so are his thoughts and opinions. And, as a de facto celebrity, everything is potentially recorded. Worse, in the digital age, anything he says can be transmitted instantly through any number of social networks to millions of cyber-peepers.

Interestingly, people make unflattering comments about other people thousands of times a day on Facebook, Twitter, or some other social network, but they usually pass without incident. Why? Because, the comments are usually made by regular folks who barely have two nickels to rub together. Threats of libel or slander against people without assets are generally meaningless because there is nothing to gain.

However, should the comment be tied to a CEO, or a high-profile attorney, or a professional athlete, or anyone with wealth, all bets are off. Defamation lawsuits have proliferated almost as quickly as the spread of social media, and judgments or settlements easily run into the millions.

WHAT EXACTLY IS DEFAMATION?

Defamation is a term used interchangeably with *libel* and *slander*. Libel is a published form of defamation, and slander is the verbal form. Whether written or spoken, defamation, or defamation of character, is when false information is represented as a stated fact. But, in order for it to be considered defamation, the information must be damaging enough to bring harm to a person or organization, and it must have been disseminated to at least one other person besides the victim.

So, in Robert's case, if he had made the comment to his opponent's face in private, it would not be considered defamation. But the fact that he made the comment in front of an audience, and that it caused harm to his opponent's reputation, meant that he opened the doors for a lawsuit. Interestingly, if there was proof that his opponent's "revolving door" actually did exist or it was already public knowledge, there would be no defamation. But alluding to it out of a hunch or some rumors with no concrete evidence to back it up is certain to draw a lawsuit.

Double Trouble

The high-profile, high net worth person's risk exposure is further multiplied by what is called the *doctrine of joint and several liability*. That means that if more than one defendant is responsible for the defamation, any one of them can be held liable. This provides the claimant with the opportunity to go after the person with the highest net worth even if he wasn't the most at fault.

For example, a CEO and his teenaged son attend a public event where they are greeted by a group of business journalists. While the CEO is engaged with a couple of the journalists, the son strikes up a conversation with two others. The son is asked how his father feels about a hostile takeover bid made by one of his fiercest competitors. Innocently, the son tells the reporters, "My dad would never allow his company to be bought by a 'drunken philanderer.'" Of course, the reporters go nuts and the quote finds its way into the newspapers and all across the Internet.

Although the CEO father was never heard to say those words, the doctrine of *vicarious liability* imposes the responsibility upon one person for the acts of another with whom the person has a special relationship. Technically, the son committed the slander, but the father is the person who will be sued.

Speaking of teenaged sons, for every person in the high net worth household who has access to social networking sites, such as Facebook, MySpace or Twitter, the odds of risk multiply. There are countless cases of parents being sued for the acts of their children on the Internet. Just last year, a teenager from Oceanside, New York, sued four of her high school classmates and their parents for $3 million. The kids were allegedly cyberbullying her, posting derogatory remarks and falsehoods.

PROFESSIONAL LIABILITY

Even though you will retire from your profession one day are you ever fully retired? Perhaps there is that desire to keep helping people solely based on your years of knowledge and experience even though you no longer have your business. Let's consider the following example. A very successful stockbroker retired at the ripe old age of 50 and decided to go into a completely different line of business. In social settings he still enjoyed talking stocks with his buddies and, when asked, he was always willing to share his top stock picks. One of his buddies acted on one of his stock picks and wound up losing $150,000. His buddy sued him for negligence in recommending an unsuitable investment. He won in court.

Even though the retired stockbroker had no intention of selling or buying stocks for clients again, he still maintained his securities licenses; however, he let his "errors and omissions" coverage lapse. As a licensed securities broker, he was still liable for any advice he rendered, but the lapse of his coverage exposed him personally to the damages caused by his advice. Doctors, lawyers, financial advisors, and accountants all have the same exposure when they dispense advice after letting their professional indemnity insurance expire.

THE HIGHER THE PROFILE, THE BIGGER THE LAWSUITS

It's not so easy being rich. At least that's how one might interpret the general feelings of high net worth individuals who responded to the ACE Private Risk Services Survey on Personal Liability Perceptions and Behavior among Wealthy Households conducted in 2011.[11] According to the survey, more than two-thirds of the high net worth community ($5 million of assets and above) believes that the public perception of the wealthy has become much more negative in the last few years. More than half of high net worth people believe that their wealth makes them a target for lawsuits, and nearly 40 percent think that increased public resentment has made them even bigger targets.

When asked what their greatest concern is about being sued, they were less concerned with losing a meaningful amount of assets (17%) than they were with the amount of time and stress that would be required to mount a legal defense (27%). And they were more worried about the expense of defending themselves (26%) than they were about the possibility their insurance wouldn't cover a potential judgment (13%). These results seem to indicate that high net worth individuals are more confident in their capacity to cover the costs of a potential lawsuit than in their ability to cope with the strain of having to defend themselves.

So it shouldn't be a surprise that the survey revealed that more than half of the respondents grossly underestimate the potential cost of a liability lawsuit. Given a scenario in which someone suffers a serious injury as the result of an accident occurring on the respondents' property, more than half said that the highest amount of damages they could be liable for is $5 million. Compared to some recent verdicts and settlements, their lowball estimate clearly demonstrates a lack of real-world awareness of the expanding appetite for jumbo awards:

- $49 million awarded to a college student left in a coma following a multivehicle crash
- $31 million awarded to two people swept off a boat and injured by its propellers
- $29 million awarded to a 4-year-old boy for a spinal cord injury resulting from a vehicle crash
- $21 million awarded for the death of a female student killed in an auto accident

- $20 million awarded for the death of a teenage boy killed when riding an ATV on a neighbor's property
- $15 million awarded to a 14-year-old boy who suffered moderate brain damage in an auto accident

Aside from the eight-figure size of these judgments, the one thing they all had in common is that the defendants all had deep pockets. Given that more than 40 percent of the respondents had less than $5 million in liability coverage or no coverage at all (4% weren't sure how much coverage they had), and only 20 percent had coverage of $10 million or more, it's safe to say that that the assets of a vast majority of high net worth individuals are dangerously exposed.

This deficiency is all the more disconcerting considering the reasons why high net worth individuals haven't obtained personal umbrella liability coverage. Of the 21 percent who don't have additional personal umbrella liability coverage, 34 percent said they were advised by their agent that they didn't need it, 37 percent said the risk is not worth the added expense, and 14 percent said that their agent recommended it but they were willing to take their chances.

That more than two-thirds of the high net worth community doesn't understand the extent of their exposure or drastically underestimates it is understandable; that's the reason I wrote this book—because it's beyond the range of their knowledge and focus to fully appreciate the extent of their exposure. However, to learn that more than three-quarters of the respondents were given advice by an agent that resulted in their not purchasing enough coverage or any coverage at all is disturbing. Granted, most mass-market property and casualty agents aren't much more informed than their clients on the risk exposures and solutions for high net worth individuals; but considering that three-quarters of wealthy individuals consult with a financial advisor or attorney on one or more elements of their financial plan, the lack of any discussion of a risk management strategy seems to be a serious oversight.

THE WEALTHY NEED TO PREPARE FOR THE WORST

Whether high net worth individuals seek them out on their own, or are referred to them by a financial advisor or attorney, independent insurance brokers specializing in risk management are the best resource with the knowledge and ability to address all of the liabilities and areas of exposure facing the wealthy today. First, a qualified risk management specialist will recommend that you prepare for a worst-case scenario initially by purchasing enough umbrella liability coverage to cover your current net worth and the present value of your employment income stream. The incremental cost of adding sufficient liability coverage is minuscule compared with the increased amount of risk exposure.

Second, a personal liability insurance plan should be coordinated with any asset-shielding trusts and techniques already in place.

Third, all of the components of your liability protection, including your home, auto, watercraft, professional, and umbrella, should be coordinated under one roof in order to avoid gaps in coverage and to ensure consistency in your legal defense efforts.

Finally, you should create an expansive preemptive strategy for reducing your exposure in all aspects of your personal and business lives. Following a complete assessment of your lifestyle needs and accompanying risk exposures, your strategy should be to enlist a safety expert to review your home and property, a security expert to install a comprehensive home security system, an investigative expert to conduct extensive background checks on employees and contractors, and a cyber-security expert to install equipment and procedures for locking down cyber-leaks. All of these experts should be retained for monitoring and upgrading systems as needed.

All of this can seem daunting, but if even the possibility exists that all of what you have worked for can suddenly be taken away, these steps could be the single best investment you can ever make. These essential steps to protecting your wealth can be made less daunting with the assistance of an experienced risk management specialist whose responsibility it is to find the most effective solutions available at the best overall value.

YOU ARE YOUR BRAND, SO YOU'D BETTER PROTECT IT

While most high net worth individuals shun the limelight, it is cast upon them by virtue of their wealth and their position in society. Those whose lives are on display by virtue of their notoriety—CEOs, high-profile professionals, investment managers, athletes and entertainers—are more conscious of their visibility. In any case, like it or not, intentional or not, each high net worth individual or family is a brand unto themselves.

Ultimately, your brand is the sum of all that is you as you perceive it, and, to a great extent, you control your brand. Your brand is also what other people perceive of you. But it's your reputation that gets left behind for others to shape on the basis of what they see and hear. And, if you aren't paying attention, your reputation may take on a far different form from the brand you want to portray. It takes a lifetime to build a reputation, but, in a world in which information travels at digital speed, it can take a matter of seconds to ruin it; and that can be more costly than any other risk exposure you might have.

Through your work, your community involvement, your philanthropy, your family achievements, and your social life, you are constantly building your brand. If you are conscious of your brand, the transparency of social media is your greatest asset, but it can also be your worst nightmare if you are not proactively managing your reputation. It takes just one rant by a disgruntled employee on Facebook, or one embarrassing picture post capturing a past moment of youthful indiscretion, to change the conversation about you. Heck, if someone really wanted to trash you, he could set up a dedicated website and have it ranked at the top of Google in one day.

Suddenly, reputation management has become a necessity for anyone who has a brand to protect. This has spawned a whole industry of services that will sweep the web of any negative history on your behalf and monitor ongoing activity. It's this millennium's version of tattoo removal for people who need to be able to put their best face forward.

Companies can now purchase reputation insurance, an indemnity product triggered by a PR crisis. As of this writing, reputation insurance for individuals is still on the drawing board, so the best insurance for individual or family brands is prevention, taking all available measures to reduce the opportunities for unwanted or malicious publicity. Some of the first places to look are your children's computers and their online and offline activities. They are also the face of your brand and unintended consequences can be damaging to your reputation.

For high-profile families it is strongly recommended that they create a family crisis team of advisors to be able to manage a situation before it really gains traction. The team should include a family spokesperson trained in PR and media relations.

PROTECTING YOUR INTELLECTUAL CAPITAL

Many people who have achieved success and wealth through their business have done so with their intellectual capital. What exactly is intellectual capital? This is the sum of the business's hidden assets, such as its human resources, knowledge, intellectual property, and all of the client and stakeholder relationships that bring immeasurable value to the company. In essence, it is your "secret sauce," which gives your business its competitive edge. When the recipe is lost or stolen, your business can lose most, if not all, of its value.

In simple legal terms, intellectual capital is comprised of the trademarks, licenses, brand names, and patents that are accumulated in a business. However, as commerce advances into the digital age, more and more intellectual capital is fueled by knowledge and relationships. Business today thrives on networks and partnerships, and it is often a key person or partner who holds the knowledge key. Key people can leave and partners can turn into competitors.

To give you an idea of just how valuable intellectual capital is, consider the bankruptcy liquidation of telecom giant, Nortel. It's hard assets—capital equipment, properties, towers, and subsidiaries—went for $2.5 billion, while its patents brought more than $4.5 billion.

A big mistake a lot of entrepreneurs and business owners make is they don't patent their creations, or, if they do, they patent the wrong things. For instance, if a business creates a revolutionary manufacturing process and patents it, the secret becomes accessible to your competitors. Trade secrets should remain secret. But, if the new process is meant to be marketed to the public, then it needs to be patented.

If your success and, ultimately, your wealth are inextricably tied to a trade secret, a patent, a brand, or a trademark, you should protect it as if you were guarding a vault of gold; because it is likely that it is worth far more than gold. Hire an attorney who specializes in intellectual capital.

Intellectual Property Insurance

Most general liability policies do not provide coverage for intellectual property. Without intellectual property insurance coverage, your company is, in essence, self-insuring against the risk of loss or damage. Patent insurance is a specialized form of intellectual property insurance that can indemnify your company from loss due to patent litigation. One type of coverage, referred to as *offensive coverage*, protects you, as the patent holder, and *defensive coverage* provides protection in the event your company is accused of patent infringement.

Obtaining intellectual property insurance may be more involved than obtaining a patent, but the effort is well worth it. The application and underwriting process is fairly extensive, requiring an in-depth patent search, legal opinions, and a customized proposal from the insurer stating the terms under which your intellectual property will be covered. Should you have a claim, either defensive or offensive, the insurer will investigate the claim, and, if need be, it will manage the lawsuit and any negotiated settlements.

Suffice it to say that insuring intellectual property is a complex issue that can be addressed only by an insurance broker with expertise in this particular area.

CHAPTER 10

Personal Risk Management Planning at the Next Level

Skiing with my old friend, Steve, always turns into a few days of regurgitating the iconic Clint Eastwood line: "Do you feel lucky?" This trip to Vail would be no different.

IT'S ALL DOWNHILL FROM HERE

Steve made his fortune managing money on Wall Street and ultimately decided a life pursuing the best beaches and ski areas the world has to offer would be much more fun. I am always happy to get his phone call with the invitation to the next great destination, although I always check to make sure my insurance policies are updated before going.

Standing at the top of Vail, I soak in the view across the snow-capped Rocky Mountains, my adrenaline rushing in anticipation of that question from Steve. "Let's head over to Highline," he says, followed by, "Do you feel lucky this time?"

"No luck needed," I reply. "I do recall you paid the tab last night at the Red Lion because you felt the need to eat some snow yesterday on this same trail. Same bet as yesterday?" I ask.

"You're on!" he replies with a toothy grin.

We work our way across the mountain top and arrive at the crest of Highline. This is a double diamond (extremely difficult) trail that runs under the Highline Express Lift on the Front Side of Vail. Looking down from the top, the terrain seems to roll out and fall from underneath us. The moguls look like miniature mountains, littering the trail all the way to the bottom. The snow is plentiful and the bumps on Highline are big, soft, and perfectly carved for the aggressive bump skier. This is my kind of skiing, and it's time to push it and see if Steve winds up eating snow again.

Like wily boxers eyeing each other to guess each other's move, we slowly inch our way toward the leftmost side of the trail. We each look for the set of moguls that will produce the perfect first few turns to set our rhythm for the downhill race. Steve stops and glares down the slope intently, slowly moving his head right, left, and right again, making the first few turns in his mind as he gets ready. He appears set to go, so I glide past him and head a few feet closer to the tree line. "Are you sure you want to be that close to the tree line?" he asks.

"Not to worry," I say, "this is all about risk and reward. I see a great line that will take me all the way to the bottom. You just get your money ready!" With that, I line myself up for the first few turns, pulling my goggles down and kicking some loose snow from my skis. Looking over at Steve, I see he's also ready to go. "Do you feel lucky?" I ask. "*Go!*"

Dropping into the first few turns my heart rate immediately jumps as the thrill of the bumps coming at me quickly, the snow flying, and the trees just half a turn to my left rocketed all my senses to immediate attention. A few feet to my right I can hear Steve groaning as his skis slam off the top of each mogul, and his knees are forced up toward his chest to absorb the impact. There's no time to look; I focus a few turns ahead, careful not to carve back toward the tree line. One bad turn and I'm in the meat sled for the rest of the way down. Like a gift that keeps on giving, Highline seems to continue to unfold, a never-ending sea of bumps. My legs burn and I can feel my turns starting to get sloppy. My mind urges me on, "Push harder! You can't let him win." The competitive side of me wants to push it all the way down. Turn after turn I keep up the pace until, finally, I pull up and out of my line of moguls. Steve continues his line down. Victory is his today.

As I reach the bottom it is time for the high-five. Steve asks, "What happened? We were turn for turn until halfway down."

Catching my breath, I reply, "Too much risk, not enough reward. My legs were giving out on me. I was too close to the tree line to have weak legs for the rest of the run. I preferred to take myself down the slope rather than rely on the transport services of ski patrol."

"Spoken like a risk manager." Steve says. "Get your wallet out because I am real thirsty after that run."

Not only is Steve a longtime friend, he is also a longtime client. Over the years we have worked together on plans that have reduced the amount of risk Steve faces. The evaluation of Steve's exposures and how to treat them are much like standing at the top of Highline and looking for the best way down. Which way is the most efficient? Which will have short-term benefits and long-term benefits?

With Steve's good fortune came myriad exposures, each with its own degree of risk and its own financial consequences. With each rung he climbed up the wealth ladder, the breadth of his exposures expanded as did the overall complexity of addressing them. No longer could he simply call his local property and casualty agent and buy a policy to cover a risk; his new lifestyle required a much broader, more comprehensive approach involving risk transfer, risk reduction, risk prevention, and ongoing risk assessment. Like other newly wealthy people now at the next level, Steve must take a systematic, solutions-based approach to protecting his quality of life. He needs a comprehensive, coordinated risk management plan.

THE PERSONAL RISK MANAGEMENT PROCESS

Personal risk management has been defined as the process for making and carrying out decisions that will minimize the adverse effects of an individual's or family's loss exposure. To state it even more simply: Risk management is analyzing and then acting appropriately on risk.

Because there isn't a one-size-fits-all plan that could possibly fit the unique needs of every wealthy family, risk management is a process that focuses on the problem of risk at every level of an individual family's lifestyle in order to ultimately arrive at a solution for each. Each risk calls for separate measures, which usually require separate forms of insurance. Because risks at the higher levels often require specialized methods and tools, the process involves a collaboration of various experts working under a coordinated plan in order to develop the most efficient and effective risk management plan.

There are four primary steps to the risk management process:

1. Identify and analyze loss exposures.
2. Identify and select risk management technique(s).
3. Implement chosen risk management techniques.
4. Monitor and measure the risk management program to seek improvements and adapt to changes.

Identify and Analyze Loss Exposures

In analyzing loss exposures, each risk is examined from three vantage points:

1. The value that is exposed to loss
2. The peril that could cause the loss
3. The probable financial consequences of the loss

This step in the process is carried out for each loss exposure: home, autos, collectibles, household employees, watercraft, professional liabilities, personal liabilities, family security, and so on. Each loss exposure is analyzed in light of the family's personal objectives for security and financial protection. Each will require its own safety measures, and each will require an individual risk management strategy.

Identify and Select Risk Management Techniques

Just as there is no one-size-fits-all plan for all families, there are no off-the-shelf risk management solutions for any particular loss exposure. Techniques must be examined for their effectiveness and efficiency in meeting the specific criteria and needs of each family. Techniques include risk control methods and techniques, as well as risk transfer through insurance. In most cases, the solution will include both, based on the balance the family wants to strike between reducing the risk (which can interfere with lifestyle choices) and transferring the risk (buying higher limits of coverage).

Selecting the best risk management techniques will come down to choosing the ones that best fit the family's lifestyle and provide the optimum level of protection. Equally important, any method selected needs to be integrated into the overall risk management plan to ensure that there are no gaps in coverage and that the family is not overpaying for coverage.

A comprehensive and well-coordinated risk management plan will consider four methods of treating risk:

1. *Risk avoidance:* By simply not performing an activity that carries risk, the risk can be avoided. For instance, by choosing not to purchase a motorcycle, you would avoid the risks associated with that activity. Of course, it's not possible to avoid all risks, and in many instances it might not make sense if the potential reward of an activity far outweighs any possible risk.

   Another form of risk avoidance is hazard prevention, in which potential hazards or perils are removed or mitigated. Examples would include ensuring there is solid fencing around a swimming pool to prevent toddlers from falling in, or paving an uneven walkway that invites slips and falls.

2. *Risk reduction:* This involves reducing the likelihood of a risk occurring, or minimizing the amount of a loss should it occur. Risk reduction methods have to be weighed against associated tradeoffs or alternative methods because some are either impractical or too costly. Installing an indoor sprinkler alarm system might reduce the risk of your home burning down; however, the risk reduction has to be weighed against the probability of severe water damage.

3. *Risk transfer:* Although you can't really transfer a risk, you can transfer all or part of the financial loss stemming from a risk occurrence. Each risk or financial exposure must be assessed to determine the threshold at which it doesn't make sense to self-insure the risk. At that threshold you then enter into a contractual transfer of risk by buying insurance coverage.

4. *Risk retention:* In some cases it may make sense to accept the loss from a risk, especially if the cost of insuring against the risk could ultimately be higher than the possible loss. When buying homeowners or auto insurance a decision is made as to how much risk is to be retained when choosing a deductible amount. The higher the deductible, the more risk is retained.

Implement Chosen Risk Management Techniques

As with any plan, implementation is the key to the success of a risk management plan. Strategies or techniques for each loss exposure must have their own implementation action plan. This might include installing equipment, contracting a specialist (i.e., cyber-security expert), a timeline, risk financing (insurance), and a system or process for monitoring. Again, each piece of the puzzle must fit together in a well-coordinated program to ensure there are no overlaps and no gaps.

Implementation must also include a complete indoctrination of family members and trusted advisors in the strategies and techniques used, and a clear channel of communication established among everyone involved.

Monitor and Measure the Risk Management Program to Seek Improvements and Adapt to Changes

A risk management plan is similar to a financial plan in that changing circumstances could impact the effectiveness of the plan. With a high net worth family, circumstances change as their net worth increases, or when they buy a bigger home or additional toys. Any change in lifestyle can present a new loss exposure that must be run through the risk management process.

In addition, existing strategies or techniques can always be improved, especially with advancements in technology. It is vitally important that an at-risk family continuously improve and upgrade their strategies because those who seek to harm or exploit them are always upgrading theirs.

GENERIC SOLUTIONS JUST DON'T CUT IT AT THE NEXT LEVEL

Steve, like many of my clients who are new arrivals at the next level, came to me with a patchwork of generic insurance policies and very little appreciation for the extent of his loss exposures. And who could fault him? He didn't achieve success and wealth by focusing on things he knew little about. Little did he know, however, that while he was busy amassing wealth, he was also expanding his loss exposure on many levels.

But, being a former money manager, Steve does understand risk management. He spent half his time identifying, analyzing, and implementing risk mitigation (hedge) strategies to minimize his clients' loss exposure. So, once he understood the extent of his personal loss exposure, it was no great leap for Steve to jump into the risk management process with both feet. He fully embraces the process and looks at his risk management plan as a hedge against the uncertainties of life.

At the risk of offending the masses, the one thing I can say about the wealthy is that they don't lead generic lives. They have the means to carve out a lifestyle of their choosing, which for most includes supersized homes, lots of expensive toys, high-profile activities, and lots of attention. All of this combines to create a potentially volatile cocktail of risk, needing just one more ingredient (a peril) to ignite a firestorm of costly liabilities. That's *not* a generic life, and it requires more than generic solutions to manage the inherent risks of a wealthy lifestyle. Nothing short of a comprehensive risk management program can protect the quality of life at this level.

CHAPTER 11

Would You See an MD Generalist for a Heart Transplant?

How do you know if the agent/broker you are working with is the right partner for you?

IT TAKES THREE TO TANGO

Driving to the Hamptons early on a crisp morning in late September is a bit like driving through the opening scene of a movie. With the windows down, I can smell the salt air as I gaze at the waterfront retreats of New York's elite. After driving nearly the entire length of Long Island, I finally round a corner that leads me down a small street that ends at the beachfront home I am looking for. As I park I can hear the waves of the Atlantic Ocean crashing just beyond the house. Nestled in the dunes, I find the home of Tatiana and Nick.

The stone driveway leads to a footpath neatly defined by a corridor of chest-high sea grass. As instructed by Nick, I follow the footpath around the side of the home toward the studio located next to the swimming pool. Approaching the studio, I hear the sound of music carrying across the ocean air from the open windows of the studio. It sounds like a tango. Knowing that Tatiana and Nick are professional dancers, this does not surprise me. As I walk closer, I can see them through the windows, practicing their dance routine. The door to the studio is open so I knock softly and enter. Nick acknowledges my presence with a quick wave, one that says *I will be with you soon*, while he's careful not to miss a step.

The routine I am watching is their signature dance, the Tango. Their bodies move elegantly together in well-rehearsed motions across the small studio floor. With each twist and turn, Tatiana seems to float effortlessly and freely, knowing her partner will be there. The dancers' eyes are fixed on each other with looks of passion and excitement as the music heightens and brings the tango to its last embrace. The music stops, and I provide a one-man standing ovation. Feeling privileged to have watched a couple at the top of their craft, I walk over to formally introduce myself and learn more about them.

The conversation starts with my learning about their history of dancing together. I want to know the key ingredient a couple must have to be the best in this art form. No sooner do I ask this question than I receive a rapid and coordinated response of trust. They tell me that it was trust that drew them together in dance and now in their married life. Tatiana tells me that "to dance freely, you must trust that your partner understands his role in supporting you. This trust allows me to focus my energy on expressing myself and making my dance as artistic and passionate as I can. This trust is not one-way; Nick has that same trust in me. Nick trusts that I will not hesitate in my moves, and that I will dance not just for me, but for both of us."

We move from the studio, crossing the patio by the poolside, and head toward the sliding doors that lead to the kitchen. Nick offers me fresh coffee as he picks through some papers he had out for us to discuss. Nick turns and asks a great question: "Brian, why should we do business with you and your firm?"

After a sip of coffee, and a quick moment to gather my thoughts, I respond with one word. "Trust" I answer. He looks at me quizzically, wondering where am I heading with this one-word answer. I continue with my response. "The tango Tatiana and you practice every day is a fantastic display of artistry, passion, and trust between two partners. The tango that I know and practice every day is a tango that involves *three* partners: You, as the insured, may feel the insurance dance is best performed one way, while the insurance company may wish to dance another way, and I, as your representative, step in as the third partner to orchestrate the dance between you as buyer and the company as insurer. My ultimate goal is to find the common trust of the other two partners: the insurance company, trusting it has all the information needed to accurately underwrite and insure your personal exposures, and your trust that the insurance company will provide a generous insuring agreement and pay claims with little inconvenience to you."

This tango of three began long before I met with Nick and Tatiana. The insurance company partners I work with first review how my office operates prior to accepting me as a dance partner. Do I have what it takes to bring them the client base they are seeking? Can I be trusted to provide them with all the underwriting details they need to appropriately underwrite a new account? Will I make the best representation of their brand as I meet with prospective clients? Can they trust my judgment to ask their underwriters to put up millions of dollars to insure the various homes, yachts, valuables, and liability exposures? The relationship between agent and underwriter begins with trust.

After explaining this relationship to Nick, he sees where I am heading. "My livelihood depends on the level of trust my tango partners have in me. This includes my insurance company partners and my clients. There are many other reasons to do business with me and my staff; however, trust leads the way."

Choosing the agency to work with and represent you to the insurance marketplace involves asking not only whom you can trust, but who is your best Tango partner.

WHAT YOUR PROPERTY-CASUALTY AGENT DOESN'T KNOW CAN HURT YOU

This wonderful client experience leads me into a much broader and far more critical discussion of where the high net worth family should turn to address their myriad intricate risk exposures. I can tell you right up front that the answer does not involve one single individual; rather, it involves a team of experts, much as the treatment of a cancer patient requires the combined expertise of an oncologist, a nutritionist, a rheumatologist, an organ specialist, an internist, and a medical specialist to coordinate ongoing care to ensure the risk of reoccurrence is minimized.

You might find the analogy to be somewhat "apples and oranges"; however, in both cases, known risks exist. They require a team of experts to reduce the risks, the risks are ongoing, and they can be life threatening. Let me amend that slightly. Personal risks may or may not be life threatening; however, they can be quality-of-life threatening. The primary difference is that a cancer survivor can't transfer the risk to an insurer, unless he has already done so by purchasing life insurance before any incidence of cancer.

You might also say that a cancer survivor is automatically going to have this team put together out of medical necessity, while a high net worth family may not comprehend the extent of their risk exposure, and therefore, the necessity of a risk management team. And I say you're right, except for the fact that many of my high net worth clients came to me after surviving a threat to their lifestyle or a significant financial loss due to a realized risk. They are, in a sense, "liability survivors" and they now understand the necessity of a risk management team.

The common denominator of the newly wealthy is that they typically carry their traditional attitudes, assumptions, and knowledge about personal risk into their new lifestyles. And they often bring their trusted and loyal property-casualty agent along to write bigger policies on their bigger houses and cars. So begins the dangerous divergence between middle-market solutions and the ever-expanding needs at the next level.

As I hope this book has illuminated, the gap between the risks that the typical property-casualty agent can cover and what actually exists at the next level is, just in terms of monetary exposure, as wide as the Grand Canyon. While there are always ways of transferring monetary risk, high net worth families live under constant threats from a number of sources, and, in some cases, it's not feasible or, perhaps, advisable to transfer all risk. So it becomes necessary to identify strategies that can reduce or control the risk. That's where risk management comes in.

This is not to belittle property-casualty agents. Unquestionably, they are a vital cog in the financial planning wheel, and most of them distinguish themselves with a commitment to their clients. In fact, where do you think many of us in commercial and high net worth personal lines come from? Typically, we come from the ranks of property-casualty agents who want to make a bigger difference in their clients' lives and who are willing and able to acquire the requisite knowledge and experience to offer a higher level of fee-based risk management services.

Seven Great Questions to Ask When Choosing an Insurance Representative

1. Are you a generalist or is personal risk management for high net worth families your specialty?
2. Describe your personal risk management process
3. What relationships do you have with advisors in the fields of art, jewelry, collection management, personal security, home appraisals or other specialized fields?
4. Which specialized insurance companies do you represent?
5. What professional designations have you earned that distinguish you in insurance and risk management?
6. What are the risk reducing services you and your firm provide beyond the purchase and placement of insurance?
7. How will you and your firm enhance the handling of my affairs for other members of my advisory team? (attorney, CPA/tax planner, family office manager, wealth manager, personal assistant)

IT'S NOT JUST ABOUT INSURANCE

Until the last decade or so, insurance companies and brokers could only offer high net worth clients one of two choices: Transfer their risks to them by buying insurance, or retain the risks and cover them out of their own wealth. More recently, an industry has emerged that offers true risk management strategies designed to help the wealthy avoid, reduce, or control their risks on a personalized basis. Pioneering insurers such ACE Private Risk Services, AIG Private Cleint, Chubb, and Fireman's Fund began allocating substantial resources toward creating a complete suite of personal risk management services for high net worth families.

While each of these insurers employs professionals with considerable loss-prevention experience, they have also developed relationships with carefully vetted third-party professionals who provide highly specialized expertise. In some instances, insurers provide policyholders access to services provided by such experts on a complimentary basis; and in other instances, the insurer has negotiated substantial discounts for its policyholders to utilize the products or services being offered. The range of risk management services that are available can be categorized in these critical areas:

- Protecting residential exposures
- Travel safety
- Managing personal staff
- Managing collections
- Family safety
- Protecting personal information

This transformative development in managing personal risks has attracted a new breed of insurance brokers who understand that purchasing insurance is only a small part of the risk management process. These insurance professionals pursue a rigorous training and work a number of years to gain the trust of these insurers in order to gain access to their exclusive, high-end suite of personal and commercial lines of insurance products. And they must continuously win their trust by building their reputation as world-class providers of the type of service that the wealthy have come to expect.

The work of an insurance broker who specializes in risk management products and services is not always as glamorous as one might imagine when working in the world of the rich and famous. While it's true that we work with some very-high-profile people, and we mix with the upper echelons of society and entertainment, a lot of our work involves digging in the weeds to assist our clients with some of the most mundane tasks. To us, it is not only a big part of our job; it is the complete top-to-bottom, 24/7, 365 days/year service that we promise our clients.

For example, just last month I had to advise my clients on a wide-ranging number of issues that had little to do with the purchase of an insurance policy. Here's just a few of the ways I helped my clients last month:

- Helped a client avoid the $.70-per-pound liability limitation in a moving contract while getting the moving company to waive the exclusion for breakage of fragile items.
- Negotiated a home-remodeling contract to have the builder take on most of the liability for structural damage.
- Warned a client giving a wedding reception for his daughter about assuming the hosting restaurant's liability for food poisoning.
- Provided a client with a trusted source for professional drivers to drive his elderly parents car reducing their risk of an auto accident.

These are just a few small examples of how I work with my clients each day to reduce their risk and save them a substantial amount of money on risk transfer. On a larger scale, I might spend hours counseling a client on his or her entire insurance portfolio. That might include reviewing everything from group policies and out-of-state vacation home coverage to policies purchased through other insurance agents. Of course, I will make recommendations where gaps clearly exist or where coverage is inappropriate.

After spending several hours assessing a client's risks and reviewing his or her policies, the only recommendations I made at the time were to increase the personal umbrella coverage by $5 million and add contingent Workers Compensation coverage for home remodeling. The commissions I earned on the sale of the insurance products barely worked out to an hourly minimum wage. My clients value me for authentic, objective advice delivered without conflict and with their interests first.

Although I am compensated for my risk management services, when I do need to recommend an insurance purchase, I do so with the capacity to network my requirements among the industry's biggest and best insurers in the high- and ultra high net worth markets, both nationally and internationally.

More important, I serve as personal advocates for my clients in the claims process where appraisal and arbitration clauses can trip them up, or when they are unjustly denied or underpaid. I step in to help the client resolve the disputes and help make the case for the claims departments to reconsider their positions. Only a handful of personal insurance companies specialize in this market—ACE Private Risk Services, AIG Private Client Group, Chubb, and Fireman's Fund are the most prominent. My recommendations are based on a complete market analysis of available solutions that consider only your specific needs.

Should your risk assessment determine that additional services are needed, such as complimentary background checks, assistance with preemptive planning for hurricanes, or designing a risk management strategy for moving an art collection across the country, I work with the insurance company and specialty service providers to do everything possible to safeguard your family and your possessions.

ADVANTAGES OF CONSOLIDATING YOUR PERSONAL RISK PROGRAM

I mentioned an example of a client for whom I spent considerable time reviewing his insurance portfolio. While I may have made only a couple of immediate recommendations to fill some glaring gaps in coverage, ultimately I recommended that they consolidate all of their insurance with just one insurance broker to make it more effective, more efficient, and far less cumbersome for everyone involved.

Avoiding the Risk of Coverage Gaps

It is likely that you have your auto insurance coverage with an auto insurer and your umbrella liability policy with another company (especially if it has more than a $1 million limit). In that situation, you run the risk of having the wrong underlying limits. If both policies are with one insurer, it will probably make the necessary adjustments; however, if they are issued through separate carriers, that responsibility falls on your shoulders.

While it's not always possible to have all of your insurance policies issued through one carrier, you can have the services of a qualified insurance broker available to monitor and adjust your coverage when necessary. But, where possible, I will recommend that all underlying policies are issued from the same company that issues the personal umbrella policy. This reduces the headaches of managing multiple insurers (the single issuing company assumes the responsibility of coordinating coverage). More important, it reduces the risks of improper coverage.

Avoiding Coverage Incongruence

Liability policies issued by different insurers are likely to have varying definitions and exclusions, which creates the potential for an incongruence of coverage. For instance, a lawsuit covered by an underlying policy may not be covered by the umbrella policy. However, an insurance broker with access to coverage that is universally broader than the standard liability, auto, or homeowners policy can eliminate the incongruence risk. But this requires constant vigilance over a client's insurance portfolio with the resources and expertise to monitor and maintain congruence.

Avoiding Overpaying for Underinsuring

According to the Ace Private Risk Services survey, "Wealth at Risk: How High Net Worth Families Overpay to Be Underinsured," June 2010, wealthy families who purchase insurance from middle-market carriers often lack adequate liability coverage, and they underinsure their custom homes and valuables collections. The survey also revealed that they are probably overpaying for their insurance because their agents don't advise them how to balance deductibles with risk exposure, and they don't always work with their clients to obtain package discounts on multiple policies. There is also a lack of loss-prevention advice, which can generate premium credits.

Here are just some of the ways the survey found that high net worth families are missing significant cost savings:

- *Raising deductibles:* 81 percent of agents surveyed report the wealthy have homeowners and auto insurance deductibles that are too low.
- *Obtaining package discounts:* 62 percent say the rich don't take full advantage of reductions for purchasing multiple policies from a single carrier.
- *Applying loss-prevention credits:* 50 percent believe that the affluent overlook adjustments for safety devices, such as burglar alarms and water-leak detection systems.

Of course, the costs of overpaying for insurance, though they can be significant, pale in comparison to the financial exposure of underinsuring or the incongruence of liability coverage. This can leave a high net worth family with hundreds of thousands of dollars—perhaps millions—of exposure. And, unfortunately for many newly wealthy families, it takes an incident for which they thought they were properly covered to expose their vulnerability.

The biggest advantage of working through a single source for all of your personal risk management needs is the benefit of highly personalized, tailored solutions that are designed around your lifestyle. Your personal risk insurance broker will know your risk profile, your preferences, priorities, and lifestyle needs better than anyone, perhaps even better than you. Specialized insurance brokers immerse themselves in your passions. It's not uncommon for them to attend the same events, participate in the same charities, or join in on the same passions enjoyed by their clients. To that extent, specialized insurance brokers are in the best position not only to protect the unique lifestyles of their clients—they also ensure their clients have access to the best risk management products and services.

SERVICE FIT FOR KINGS AND QUEENS

Who doesn't like to be treated like royalty every now and then? That's why we like to fly first-class and enjoy five-star resorts. While high-net-worth families may not live like royalty, they have worked hard to develop a quality of life to which they have grown accustomed. It would be hard for any family to have to adjust to a lower quality of life for having been displaced from their home. But, it can be especially hard for a family used to living in a large, custom home, especially if it is for an extended period of time. That's why the high-end specialized carriers provide their high net worth clients with tailored claims services that cater to their unique needs.

I can cite several cases in which clients were displaced from their homes due to a fire or natural disaster, and Chubb or AIG stepped in to quickly find them a rental home of equivalent size and comfort. And, after an accident, these specialized insurers would never allow their clients to drive anything less than the type of car that matches their taste in vehicles.

The rash of natural disasters over the past couple of years has put specialty insurers to the test in serving their high net worth clients; however, because specialized coverage is already tailored to the unique situations of their clients and their higher exposures, the custom-made solutions are already in place when disaster strikes. For example, with Superstorm *Sandy*, the most expensive storm in terms of liabilities to hit the United States, many people who carried standard homeowner policies were fighting for the limited loss-of-use coverage these insurers provide. Homeowners with specialized insurance were provided with unlimited loss of use coverage allowing them to maintain their standard of living while their home was being repaired. You can be sure that, after *Sandy*, more homeowners are looking into specialized insurance.

But it's everything that happens behind the scenes and on behalf of the client that is especially impressive. At the moment a loss is reported a whole team of insurance specialists are assigned and some will immediately converge on the scene. Essentially, they take over everything from making relocation arrangements to bringing in water and fire remediation firms to communicating with contractors and other vendors. In essence, they put on their white gloves so their clients don't have to lift a finger. Real royalty might get better service, but not by much.

IT TAKES A VILLAGE

In the spirit of full disclosure, I am a specialized insurance broker. I do work extensively with the aforementioned risk management firms to provide a full range of personal risk products and services to my clients. And, while my background, experience, and knowledge certainly qualifies me to be entrusted with the protection of my clients' lifestyles, I can only solve for one piece of the puzzle. No single advisor, no matter how trusted, can or should undertake the massive responsibility for ensuring the ultimate safety and security of their clients. Rather, it takes a team approach in which all advisors must play a vital role.

Pulling the Advisory Team Together

Most high net worth individuals are surrounded by a small cadre of advisors—a financial advisor, an attorney, an insurance professional, an accountant, and business planning specialists—each tasked with solving a different piece of the puzzle for their client. However, without coordination or collaboration among the various disciplines, the client could be left holding different pieces of the puzzle without a clear picture of how they fit together.

We all know what it's like to try to piece together a puzzle without being able to see the box-top. And, because each of the pieces is formed in separate silos, they probably won't fit cleanly together, if at all, leaving you, at best, confused and unsettled, and, at worst, with some serious gaps in the risk management plan.

High net worth individuals and families need an integrated approach to their risk management planning, but most don't know how to achieve it on their own. This requires a collaborative process that incorporates the planning efforts of multiple disciplines and a coordinated plan. Put another way, it requires a team approach that is championed by a professional advisor who is adept at forging effective, working relationships with advisors in other disciplines.

In the case of a risk management plan, the advisor in the best position to function as the team quarterback is the specialized insurance broker. Whoever is selected as the team leader, he or she assumes the responsibility for ensuring that all of the elements of the plan are developed as prescribed by the risk assessments, and that the plan is then fully implemented on an established timeline.

- The attorney

   The attorney oversees all contracts and legal agreements associated with the risk management plan. He or she is often involved in the negotiations alongside the specialized insurance broker. He also ensures that the risk management strategies are integrated with other aspects of the client's legal affairs.
- The financial advisor

   The client's primary financial advisor should be well-versed in matters of personal risk management. And where a potential vulnerability exists, the advisor should be able to identify it and refer the client to a specialized insurance broker. The financial advisor is positioned to track the client's net worth and to determine whether an adjustment in coverage limits may be necessary due to changes in portfolio values.
- The certified public accountant (CPA)

   In many cases, the CPA is positioned as the primary advisor for determining financial exposure based on assets and income. The risk management specialist or specialized insurance broker should work closely with the client's CPA or tax professional to ascertain the client's precise financial risk at all times.
- The specialized insurance broker

   At the outset, the specialized insurance broker should initiate the collaboration of the client's team of advisors for the purpose of enlisting and indoctrinating them into the risk management process. As part of that collaboration, the specialized insurance broker should establish the lines of communication and a regular review process with the team.
- Business planning specialist

   The business planning specialist and the insurance broker should have a direct line of communication to ensure congruence between business liability coverage and personal lines coverage. Any substantial changes in business structure, the balance sheet, business or product lines, capital acquisitions, travel requirements, employee procedures, vendor and client relationships, and so forth, should be communicated to the insurance broker to assess risk exposure.

■ Risk management specialist

The risk management specialist—both business and personal—provides continuous services to identify, analyze, and treat risk exposures while overseeing the implementation and monitoring of risk management strategies. He or she is responsible for ensuring that the right assets are in place to provide the tightest possible security and to reduce or control risks to the greatest extent possible. The risk management specialist and the insurance broker work hand-in-hand in the implementation of risk management strategies.

Some clients with extraordinary needs find comfort in utilizing a knowledgeable insurance broker versed in both insurance coverage and personal risk management along with an outside risk management firm specializing in personal risk analysis to act as their eyes and ears in managing the relationship with the insurance broker.

These advisors form the core of the risk management team; however, a number of other advisors or individuals can be involved, depending on the specific situation and risk exposure. The key is that there must be a well-coordinated, collaborative approach to risk management to ensure the broadest amount of protection, the tightest security, and the greatest peace of mind for my clients.

CHAPTER 12

Getting Started with Next-Level Planning

Anyone who was connected to the world via their televisions on the afternoon of January 15, 2009, will never forget the "Miracle on the Hudson," the now-immortalized act of heroism by U.S. Air Flight 1549 Captain "Sully" Sullenberger. While selfless acts of heroism occur every day across the country, the "Miracle" will always epitomize the personal intrepidness that Americans hold in the highest esteem. The "perfect" emergency landing of the Airbus A320, carrying 155 passengers, on the frigid Hudson River in full view of the West Side of Manhattan, was nothing short of spectacular.

Was it really a miracle? Or was it a perfect example of risk management in action where all risks and contingencies were expertly identified, assessed, planned, and prepared for with all available instruments and techniques implemented to minimize the greatest possible risks?

Consider this:

- With nearly 35,000 hours of flight time between them, Captain Sullenberger and First Officer Skiles had acquired the skills and judgment to handle just about any situation, and they had trained extensively on emergency water landings.
- The flight crew was highly trained in emergency situations—enough to know that only the front doors of the aircraft should be opened in a water landing. They actually prevented a passenger from opening the rear doors, which would have caused the aircraft to fill with water.
- The A320 is fully engineered to withstand a water landing, all the way down to the ditch button, which, when pressed just before the plane hits the water, will fully seal the fuselage, thereby slowing the inflow of water into the aircraft. This is what enabled the plane to stay afloat as long as it did, allowing all passengers and crew to get off safely. In addition, the A320's emergency power generator, installed for just these

contingencies, enabled the pilots to continue to control the plane after the engines shut down.

- The response on the ground and in the water was equally remarkable, involving New York and New Jersey police officers and fire crews, Coast Guardsmen, EMTs, and other responders—all of whom have trained endlessly for this exact situation.

As much as I would like to believe in miracles, the enormous amount of preemptive planning, preparing, training, and engineering that go into managing the risks of air travel played a significant role in turning what could have been a devastating loss into a chilling inconvenience for the 155 passengers.

For all the layers of protection and the myriad risks it seeks to address, personal risk management planning is much less complex than managing the risks of air travel; yet, it is still seen by many high net worth individuals and advisors as more trouble than it is worth. Of course, that's the way the high net worth community viewed comprehensive financial planning just 30 years ago—"too daunting," "not necessary," or "it can wait"—when it was introduced by a relatively small number of financial planners. Today, there are more than 300,000 financial advisors clamoring to provide comprehensive financial planning for the wealthy, who now recognize how essential it is for building and preserving their wealth.

Today, personal risk management planning is not exclusive to high net worth individuals; it is practiced by a relatively exclusive group of specialized insurance companies, firms, and independent insurance brokers. Other advisors, such as family offices, wealth managers, and attorneys, have only recently begun to get on board, integrating at least the discussion of risk management into their respective planning processes.

So the fact that most of the high net worth community has yet to engage in a comprehensive process to develop a personal risk management plan is not surprising. It's a new discipline that represents a changing world and forces an uncomfortable admission that we've entered a "new normal" in which personal safety and wealth protection have become paramount in order to survive. It's a natural human inclination to turn inward and try to ignore the 800-pound gorilla in the room, even though it will never go away.

IT'S NOT GOING TO GET ANY EASIER

Living as we do in the most tumultuous and rapidly evolving period in our history, uncertainty reigns all around us. The threats to our wellbeing increase in proportion to our net worth. The growing income disparity and resentment of the "haves" will only lead to more incidences of extortion and kidnapping, especially as these crimes become more institutionalized in organized syndicates. As global strife continues to fuel a shrinking world on fire, the wealthy will wear ever-expanding targets on their backs. The "have-nots" have learned that the quickest path to wealth redistribution is through a tort system that facilitates the legal looting of the wealthy, forcing an upward surge in multimillion-dollar settlements.

No, it's not going to get any easier to move up the wealth ladder; and those who, through a lack of knowledge, or awareness, or humility, fail to adequately prepare could suffer potentially severe consequences that could have been minimized or avoided. Unlike investing in the stock market, in which there is a fairly predictable ebb and flow of risk, personal risks among the wealthy will only continue to increase in unpredictable ways. Interestingly, most wealthy investors understand the use of risk mitigation techniques to protect their portfolios, but they have yet to grasp the severity of risks that could possibly take away everything they have worked tirelessly to create.

HOW DO YOU EAT AN ELEPHANT?

After painting that somewhat gloomy picture of the future, obviously designed to spur you to action, let me be the first to dispel any notion that effective risk management has to be the daunting, resource-intensive experience this book may have led you to believe. Yes, there are myriad risks that have to be addressed, and there could be a dozen or more layers of protection that need to be implemented, but the process doesn't have to be overwhelming or even costly. In fact, the most effective way to plan and implement a personal risk management program is to take one bite at a time and implement it gradually over time.

When I first met many of my clients, they had at least some sense of the innumerable risks they faced. But they were paralyzed with confusion and overwhelmed with the prospect of having to solve for each one of them. It was as if they had a box full of puzzle pieces but no idea of how to put the puzzle together because they were missing the box-top. Have you ever tried putting together a puzzle without the box-top? If you have, you probably abandoned the effort after about five minutes. My clients had a box full of risks, but they didn't have the big picture to help them understand where they fit on the risk spectrum or how interconnected they were.

The first step in the personal risk management process is to create the box-top so we can begin to fit the pieces of the puzzle together. Then, as we do with most puzzles, we want to start with the biggest piece because that will make it easier to complete the puzzle, right?

So, in following the risk management process I described in Chapter 10, we build the box-top by identifying and analyzing all loss exposures to determine which have the greatest likelihood of occurring and which could have the greatest impact on your financial resources. In essence, we prioritize the risk exposures and look for the biggest (most threatening) pieces.

The second step is to decide which piece to solve, which is typically going to be the biggest piece, and continue with the remainder of the risk management process:

1. Identify and analyze loss exposures.
2. Identify and select the best risk management technique(s).
3. Implement chosen risk management techniques.
4. Monitor and measure the risk management program to seek improvements and adapt to changes.

Taking the biggest bite, we then identify and examine all available risk management techniques that apply, including risk control and risk financing methods. The former might entail risk avoidance or risk reduction strategies, and the latter will typically involve either risk retention (self-insuring) or risk transfer (purchasing insurance).

That's it. We're done, until you decide to solve for the next piece of the puzzle, or through my ongoing risk assessment it's determined that a risk has increased in severity and I suggest immediate action. As each piece of the puzzle is solved, your risk protection increases as does your peace of mind. But you (or the circumstances) will dictate how quickly the puzzle comes together.

GO AHEAD AND RIP OFF THAT BAND-AID!

I remember as a kid leaving a Band-Aid on as long as I could because I couldn't bear the pain of removing it. And, no matter how much my mother insisted that it would take just a millisecond to rip it off and that the pain would last just a second more, I insisted on leaving it on until it would fall off by itself. Little did I know that when a Band-Aid is left on a wound too long a lot can go wrong. It can slow the healing, it can trap bacteria, leading to infection—not to mention the adhesive can bond to the skin, which reduces the chances of its falling off by itself and increases the pain factor. I now know that ripping it off sooner rather than later is not only less painful, it's actually better for the healing process.

Sorry to drag you through this painful analogy, but while it may be overly simplistic, its application here is airtight (sorry). In just about anything we do in life that requires some brief, initial pain and suffering in order to improve our lot, the longer we avoid it, the more difficult it becomes to take that critical first step. I'm not saying the risk management planning process itself is painful. Except for the investment of time up front, it's really not. But it can open a wound that people have tried to keep covered, namely the realization of just how vulnerable they really are. But once the process rips off the Band-Aid, the risk of infection begins to go away. Okay, I've beaten this analogy to death.

CHAPTER 13

Making the Move Abroad

In the spring of 1992, I received some news that was music to my ears. My brother-in-law's company was transferring him to Genoa, Italy, for three years. It was crushing for my parents as it meant their only daughter would be far from home. For me, it meant a place to crash while taking in the sights of Italy and enjoying summer days on the Italian Riviera. In August 1992, I made my first trip to visit with the new expatriate couple.

The directions my sister provided sounded easy enough. Take a flight from New York to Rome and then catch a connection to Genoa where she would meet me at the airport. Upon arrival, and much to my surprise, I was met by my sister driving my brother-in-law's Honda Prelude, Florida license plates and all! The sight of this puzzled me as much as it puzzled the Italians, who would invariably point to the car and comment on the Florida license plates. Every trip in the Honda turned into a game of counting how many heads turned and fingers pointed at the sight of the little white Honda with Florida plates.

I was excited to be in Italy, but little did I know then that I was getting my first lesson in what it meant to be an expatriate. For my brother-in-law, this was his opportunity to show the top executives at his company his understanding of managing and growing an international business. For my sister, this meant packing up life as she knew it and taking it all on a great adventure. The logistics were daunting. Most of their belongings from their Florida home had to go into long-term storage. The remaining items were packed into a cargo container, along with the Honda, and sent by sea to Genoa.

The ride from the airport to their apartment in the heart of Genoa was all of 30 minutes. For anyone who has driven 30 minutes anywhere in Italy, you know the heart-racing experience that can be. It was the middle of the day and I was looking forward to getting to the apartment so I could put my feet up for a few minutes. As she was opening the door my sister advised me not to expect a palatial space like their home in Florida. When I walked in I realized this was no exaggeration. The apartment had two bedrooms, a good-sized living room, a tiny kitchen, one bathroom, and a few balconies with a magnificent vantage point to gaze across the rooftops of the city. But it also had many of the comforts from Florida they had brought with them. From bedding to wardrobes, couches to clocks, audio/video systems to paintings, it had become their home-away-from-home.

IT'S ALL IN THE PLANNING

Like thousands of others who head abroad as part of a career move or simply for a change of scenery, my sister and brother-in-law spent many months planning to ensure a smooth transition. This planning included many personal risk management steps that everyone moving abroad needs to consider. Expatriates face many challenges when it comes to living abroad. There are unfamiliar legal systems, language barriers, cultural norms that come into play when determining liability, and potential hostility from locals, all of which can add up to trouble if not properly understood and fully factored into their plans.

Just like in the home country, valuable articles need to be scheduled and named in the insurance policy, insured up to their true value. However, once secured, the insurance should work worldwide. For example, the theft of a diamond ring in the host country, home country, or even while traveling to a third country would be fully covered if the item was properly scheduled with the insurance company beforehand.

WHAT EVERY EXPATRIATE SHOULD KNOW ABOUT INTERNATIONAL INSURANCE COVERAGE

We are all familiar with the preparation that takes place before we take the family away for the long weekend or summer getaway? The bills are paid up, e-mails and voicemails changed, doors locked at home, and perhaps even ask the post office to hold the mail delivery for a few days. Now multiply these as your family moves thousands of miles away for a few years as part of your career move. What do you need to prepare for this move?

The Home Back Home

The very first consideration for executives heading abroad is what to do about the homes they're leaving behind. Should the home be rented to others while they are away? Should the home be left unoccupied with a neighbor, friend, or caretaker occasionally looking after it? For many, selling the property is not an option because this is the home and community they wish to return to at some point. Let's look at the two items that deserve the attention of personal risk management: renting the home to others and leaving the home vacant and/or unoccupied.

Renting the Home to Others

Being a landlord is difficult enough when the property is located next-door or within a short distance of your home; when it's located thousands of miles away, many of the challenges can be magnified. Understanding what a homeowners policy will and won't do is critical to ensure you're not left exposed to paying a claim out-of-pocket.

Frank, an accounting executive, contacted me to ask questions about his home policy and renting the home to others. Frank and his wife, Lisa, live in a stately home on Long Island in a very desirable neighborhood. When offered a transfer to Japan to head up the Tokyo office, he jumped at the opportunity. He saw it as an experience that would surely open doors to more senior positions when he returned to New York after a four-year stint. Several weeks prior to contacting me, Frank and Lisa consulted with a local realtor about renting their home. Within two weeks, the realtor had three highly qualified candidates interested in renting the home. Frank wanted to know if the current homeowners policy could remain in place. I quickly answered no and explained to him some of the changes that would be needed.

As a landlord there are several key areas that need to be addressed by his insurance policy and by an insurance policy the tenant must maintain. For Frank, his main risks include the rebuilding of the structure after a loss, the potential loss of rental income if a peril makes the home uninhabitable, potential personal injury issues that can arise between and landlord and tenant, and liability issues that are related to bodily injury and/or property damage. The tenant must have a renters policy to protect himself for personal liability and for the personal property he brings into the home. The lease between the landlord and the tenant should clearly spell out the tenant's responsibility for his own property, and that the tenant must provide evidence of personal liability insurance, asking the tenant to also provide evidence of a personal umbrella liability policy for an added level of protection.

Frank, already having insured the structure to its correct value, quickly understood the need to keep the amount of coverage on the structure the same. The next part of the conversation turned to the importance of personal injury coverage, which caught Frank by surprise. The language and terms of personal injury coverage were foreign to Frank. I explained to him that, by insuring his home with a company specializing in larger homes, personal injury was included on his policy. Prior to becoming a landlord, the personal injury coverage protected him for claims arising from libel and slander. Now, as a landlord, additional exposures come about that only personal injury coverage can address. These include wrongful eviction from, wrongful entry into, or the invasion of the right of private occupancy of a room, dwelling, or premises that a person occupies by or on behalf of its owner, lessor, or landlord.

Frank's next question was a good one. "What's the difference between personal injury liability and personal liability?" This is where the insurance jargon caught Frank by surprise as it does many of my clients. I explain to Frank: "Personal injury is actions viewed as damaging to the character of a person: libel, slander, wrongfully evicting a tenant. Personal liability deals with claims related to the bodily injury or property damage you cause to a third party." Frank quickly saw the difference and understood the exposure he faced as a landlord.

In addition to the liability exposures, other changes were needed, which included covering the potential loss of rental income as well as eliminating the personal property in their home as he and Lisa planned to put all their belongings into storage. These are changes to the policy the insurance company was able to accommodate, which were put into effect within a few days after Frank and Lisa left for Tokyo. For extra peace of mind they decided to increase their own personal umbrella liability policy from $5 million to $10 million. Last, Frank had his attorney draft a lease for the tenant that included provisions directing the tenant to secure his own renters policy and personal umbrella liability policy.

Often I see single-family homes that are rented to others written on commercial policy forms. This raises many concerns, including the difference in policy language between a personal policy and a commercial policy. A brief outline of these policy differences is included in the outline that follows. As you can see, there is a big difference between the forms. Keep in mind that the differences in underlying coverage provided by each of these policies also impact how your personal umbrella policy may or may not respond in the event of a severe claim.

Personal Policy vs. Commercial Policy

- The liability limit on a personal policy resets with each occurrence (claim). On commercial forms once an aggregate liability limit is reached the policy no longer responds to liability claims.
- Personal forms will often have the ability to provide personal injury (character) coverage. Commercial forms may restrict this coverage.
- Personal policies will cover the loss of rental income based on the actual loss you sustain. Commercial policies may limit this coverage.

Leaving the Home Vacant or Unoccupied

Traditional insurance companies have starkly different views of homes left vacant for a brief vacation versus homes left vacant for an extended stay overseas, and that difference often catches expatriates off-guard when something happens to their home. You could be "vacationing" in France for a month, and if you receive a call that your house back in the states suffered a couple hundred thousand dollars of fire damage, your homeowners policy will most likely have you covered. But, should you extend your stay to six months, you may find that your covered perils have gone away. Covered perils such as vandalism almost certainly disappear when your house is vacant for more than 90 days (60 days in some cases).

A surprisingly large number of expatriates leave town without fully understanding the limitations of their homeowners policy on their vacant homes. And, then there are those who rented their homes only to have their renter leave. At that moment, their home may be considered vacant and not covered for most perils under a standard homeowners policy. Other expatriates mistakenly assume that, by having a friend or relative check on the house periodically, and even stay for a short time, their homeowners coverage will still apply.

The only coverage that can fully protect your vacant home while living abroad is "expatriate vacant homeowners insurance," offered by specialty insurance carriers.

INTERNATIONAL PROPERTY COVERAGE

Your personal property coverage is also at risk. If you lose a watch while vacationing in England for a month, your valuable articles policy will cover it. It's not uncommon for expatriates to take $20,000 to $100,000 worth of personal property on their assignments and then wrongly assume their homeowners policy will protect all of it.

In many cases, expatriates will wait until they arrive in their host country to begin exploring options for covering their property and valuables. And, in most cases, they are in for a rude awakening. Chances are they will encounter one or more of the following:

- Absence of insurance carriers in the host country
- Policies written in a foreign language with terms and conditions typical for that country
- Unwillingness of insurers to work with foreigners
- Insurers with questionable reputations and/or inadequate level of coverage

Even if you can find a local insurer that will work with you, you need to consider the possibility of something happening within the host country, such as a natural disaster, political upheaval, or other catastrophic event that could make it difficult to access the services of your insurer.

VALUABLE ARTICLES VERSUS REGULAR PROPERTY

As with your standard homeowners policy, a distinction must be drawn between what the insurer considers to be your "regular" property (i.e., furnishings, clothing, electronics, etc.) and your valuables, which require a separate schedule in order to protect their full value. A new $20,000 designer sofa may be one of kind, but it is not considered to be a "valuable." Essentially, valuables are pieces of property that require an appraisal in order to determine their true value. Art, high-end jewelry, antiques, and rare wines are examples of valuables that would need a separate schedule attached to your policy.

Nothing less than expatriate or international property insurance, purchased from a specialty insurance carrier before leaving abroad will fully protect your property.

As with standard homeowners policies your valuables need to be scheduled and named in the policy so they can be insured up to their true value. Above all else, you need to make sure that a lost diamond ring is covered, not only in the host country, but in any third country you may visit as well. This requires specialized coverage with the proper scheduling of your property.

SCHEDULING YOUR VALUABLES

We covered in detail the scheduling of valuables and collectibles in Chapter 3; however, it bears repeating here because protecting your property overseas requires separate and specific international property coverage.

Items valued at $5,000 or more require a separate, valid appraisal in order to be scheduled. For an appraisal to be valid, it must meet certain criteria:

- Each item requires its own appraisal document that specifies the value and date of the appraisal.
- The appraisal must be signed by a certified appraiser and include the business name and the title of the appraiser.
- The appraisal must include specific details of the item down to weight, size, composition, artist or creator, age, and anything else that determines value.

STORING YOUR PROPERTY

In most cases, expatriate workers leave behind a good portion of their property to be stored in a commercial storage facility. Most storage facilities will offer their own insurance, and some require its purchase in order to store your property. Unless you can verify the coverage provided and the legitimacy of the provider, you should obtain your own storage insurance from the same insurer with whom you have your personal property coverage. Insurers that offer international property coverage can also provide storage coverage for your property across the globe.

TRANSIT INSURANCE

If there are any gaps in international property insurance, they are typically found in transit coverage for protecting your property from loss or damage on its journey. It's not uncommon for property to become damaged at some point during its loading or offloading, while in customs, or in storage while in transit. Transit insurance coverage should protect your items at any stage between your home and their ultimate destination. It's recommended that you obtain your international property insurance from a carrier that includes transit insurance. That way, the scheduling of property can carry over to the transit coverage.

Protecting your personal property overseas does not have to be any more involved than protecting it here at home except that it does require separate coverage provided by an international insurance specialty company. It is highly recommended that you purchase your coverage before relocating from a reputable company with the capability of bundling your other international coverages, such as personal liability and vacant home coverage.

INTERNATIONAL PERSONAL UMBRELLA LIABILITY COVERAGE

Hit a pedestrian while vacationing in some far-off land and your automobile policy just may protect you. Do the same thing while living abroad and you may be out of luck. Then try leaving a country in which a big judgment goes against you and you can't pay. The consequences of committing a negligent act and incurring a liability in a foreign country can be nightmarish, yet, remarkably, most expatriates ignore the importance of global liability protection.

Most expatriates assume that the deep pockets or the general liability coverage of their employer will come to their rescue. While that may be true in some cases, it's not the smartest approach for either the company or the expatriate employee. The reality is that most employers do not carry the type of coverage that will protect an employee against personal losses while on foreign assignment. And, in most cases, to pay an expatriate's claim from their deep pockets would cause most employers some legal and tax headaches they would rather avoid. Most companies expect their expatriate employees to obtain the essential personal liability coverage appropriate for living abroad.

Personal injuries can occur anywhere, and, unfortunately, many expatriates learn the hard way that foreign societies are just as litigious, if not more, than our own. Also, Americans are often shocked at the swift judgments imposed by local magistrates—no trials, no appeals—just immediate justice. In some jurisdictions, the inability to pay the damages often results in jail, prison, or maybe deportation, which may even lead to your termination by your employer.

Just trying to understand the local laws, especially as they relate to personal injury, is nearly impossible; finding yourself stranded in a country that has no qualms about slapping high net worth Americans with a six- or seven-figure damage award, the consequences can be far-reaching, possibly leading to a loss of your job and financial ruin. Global liability insurance is the most reliable solution that would cover claims against an expatriate or his or her family related to a lawsuit or damage awards due to a negligent act. And for just $20 to $30 a month, it would seem almost criminal not to buy it on your way out of town.

Getting It Right with International Liability Insurance

- Your international personal umbrella liability coverage should protect you and your family anywhere on the globe, even if you are in different countries.
- International personal umbrella insurance purchased in the host country is not likely to provide protection when you leave the host country. Your coverage should follow you anywhere, including your visits back to the United States.
- If you are sued or attached with damages for negligence, you will need local legal representation. Your employer cannot legally defend you unless it is also named in the suit.
- Your international liability coverage needs to be comprehensive in order to protect you and your family members against unintentional personal injury, bodily harm, and property damage on and off your premises.
- Your employer cannot cover your personal claims.

International Auto Coverage

Many expatriates maintain the urge to drive even on foreign roads, whether it's to commute to work or just to explore the countryside. Needless to say, having the proper international auto insurance is critical to ensure the fullest protection for you and your family. As with international liability insurance, purchasing coverage locally will not likely provide protection should you venture outside of the host country. International auto insurance issued by a specialty insurer should provide you with worldwide coverage and be able to adjust to the requirements among the countries you plan to visit. In addition, it should include transit and destination coverage for autos shipped overseas.

International Health Insurance

For too many expatriates who become injured or ill while on assignment, it comes as a shock when they find out their employer-sponsored health insurance doesn't translate easily, if at all, to foreign health-care providers. If you should become badly injured while on a drive in the country, you may not get that helicopter ride to the hospital unless you have the right international coverage.

International health insurance is specifically designed for expatriates and their families, providing worldwide medical coverage. Purchased in the same way health insurance is offered at home, international health insurance offers similar types of options for deductibles, co-pays, and coverage limits.

KEY TAKEAWAY—DON'T LEAVE HOME WITHOUT IT

At the first inkling that you're not in Kansas anymore, you had better hope you left home with the proper coverage to protect your house back home, your property abroad, your family, and your financial assets, all of which can have much greater exposure abroad than they have at home. The time to start planning, preparing, and executing a risk management strategy for living abroad is when you begin considering such a move; once you accept the offer, things begin to happen very quickly and the whole process can become overwhelming. "First-things-first" for future expatriates means putting a comprehensive risk management plan in place.

One of the more important takeaways from this is to understand that your employer is neither obligated nor equipped to provide you with the essential protections you need. Your employer should provide you with a handbook for expatriates that should alert you to the many exposures of living abroad. Your next step is to take it to an independent insurance broker who specializes in expatriate insurance protection.

CHAPTER 14

Weaving It all Together

Chapters 1 through 12 discussed several risks you may be facing. These chapters also made it clear that there are options available from specialists in the insurance industry that understand your lifestyle. These options include insurance products as well as personal risk management strategies you can implement. The case study that follows will help you see how both insurance products and personal risk management strategies helped greatly reduce the risks faced by Francesca and her family.

FRANCESCA'S FABULOUS LIFE—A CASE STUDY

Francesca has had a remarkable career. She graduated at the top of her business school class at Wharton in 1990 and interned each summer at the investment bank Fischer, Lane, and Company. As an intern, she impressed the executives so much that they had a job on the investment banking team ready for her upon graduation. There she worked her way up from summer intern to chairwoman and CEO.

Francesca quickly earned a reputation as a top performer and found herself heading the investment banking division after seven short years with the firm. She led her division to become the most profitable in the firm, which opened the path for her to the senior executive level as vice president of the investment banking goliath. During these years her annual earnings averaged $3 million and her stock options piled up.

On her 45th birthday, Francesca was nominated by the board of directors at Fischer, Lane, and Company to be the new chairwoman and CEO. She has now held this position for five years. In addition to her success as a businesswoman, Francesca also prides herself in her roles as wife, mother, philanthropist, and connoisseur of art. One of her favorite activities is the pursuit of fine paintings by upcoming artists and loaning those paintings to galleries and museums. Her husband, John, is a vintage auto enthusiast, who manages their collection of 11 vehicles. In addition, they have their daily-use vehicles, which include a BMW M5 for him and a Range Rover for her.

Most weekends, Francesca and John enjoy packing the family into the Range Rover to head to their country home in Vermont. This allows them time to reconnect with their three children and enjoy outdoor activities, such as riding their snowmobiles and quads, along with tending to their horses.

A great personal staff helps the family keep their demanding lifestyle in order. Until recently, her executive assistant, Pam, handled many of her personal affairs, including her personal risk management needs. One day I received a call from Pam, who had been instructed by her boss to "get quotes" for some insurance policies; before I could do that, I told her I needed to learn more about her boss, as well as her own knowledge of personal risk management and insurance.

Pam told me her only knowledge about insurance came from speaking with Francesca's property-casualty agents—a New York agent who began working with Francesca when she rented her first apartment in New York City, and an agent in Vermont who was referred to her by a real estate broker.

It didn't take long to determine that Pam's knowledge in personal risk management was fairly limited. Although she had the basics of insurance down pretty well, I told her that to plan properly, I would need to meet with Francesca and John so I could walk them through our personal risk management process. She understood that the details I needed to know could come only from Francesca and John, so she arranged for a meeting at their home.

I met with them a few days later at their primary residence on Long Island, in the Village of Old Brookville. I explained to them that personal risk management planning includes understanding their objectives, and learning about their lifestyle and exposures; I then would apply the risk management process to their specific exposures. The conversation and process began with the all-important question: "What are your objectives/goals when it comes to personal risk management and insurance?"

This opened a great conversation during which the couple revealed their goals and dreams. That led to a frank discussion about their biggest concerns, the risks they face and how they could impact the lifestyle they enjoy. Their objectives included transferring risk, where possible, to an insurance company or contractually back to another party. Liability suits scare them more than the loss of property. Francesca stated: "I can easily buy another car or pay a deductible, because those are small checks. My objective is to protect our lifestyle from potential liability suits and the big checks that we may be self-insured for. I want a sound program, not just a three-ring binder of policies."

I thanked Francesca and John for their frankness and explained that my job is to guide them through a process from which we craft a program to help them meet their objectives. I then explained the next step, which is for me to learn about their lifestyle. With that we began delving into their exposures through the use of a very detailed questionnaire.

The questionnaire revealed information about their homes, their vehicles, the staff they employ, the passions they pursue (art, wine jewelry, collectibles), boards on which they serve, their toys (boats, RVs, ATVs, snowmobiles, personal aircraft), and more. *This is not merely inventory taking*; rather, the goal is to get a complete understanding of all potential exposures their lifestyle presents to them.

At the conclusion of our meeting, Francesca and John thanked me and expressed their surprise at how the meeting truly opened their eyes and minds to the need for proper personal risk management. I let them know that my job had only just begun, and that I would spend a few days reviewing what I had learned about their objectives and lifestyle: "Now that I have a complete grasp of your objectives and exposures, I will begin to design a personal risk management and insurance plan for you." We planned to meet at the end of the following week, after Francesca returned from a business trip.

We convened in their vast family room the following week. With the fireplace crackling and the smell of freshly baked cookies permeating the air, I presented their plan. "Francesca and John," I began, "congratulations on the success and lifestyle your hard work has helped you achieve. Now, let's see how to best protect it."

As is typical with high net worth families who grow into their wealthy lifestyles gradually, there were myriad issues covering several areas of risk; I broke them down into a problem-and-solution format to make it easier to follow.

Protecting the Home

We began by talking about the home in Brookville—a beautiful colonial, measuring just over 5,000 square feet and sitting on two acres.

> **Problem:** The Old Brookville home, with an estimated cost to rebuild of $2,250,000, is insured for only $1,375,000, with a company lacking expertise in the high-value home market.
>
> **Solution:** Secure coverage with a company experienced in appraising and insuring high-value homes. The experts at the company I recommended visited their home to take photographs and measurements; they then provided a very detailed appraisal report about the appropriate amount of coverage necessary.

Problem: Their prior insurance company did not have the ability to provide uncapped extended replacement cost.

Solution: Obtain uncapped extended replacement cost coverage. By having the home appraised by the insurance company and insuring it for its suggested value, the company will agree to replace the dwelling, even if the cost exceeds the policy limit.

Problem: The home was originally built in 1863, and Francesca and John invested heavily to restore the home to its original grandeur and retain its historic qualities. Again, their insurer did not have the capability to properly address these needs.

Solution: Obtain coverage that will replace their historic home's special architectural and historic features with the same quality materials and workmanship.

Problem: Francesca and John's personal objectives were not taken into account with the policy in place. The deductible on the home policy was just $500, for which they were paying a very high premium.

Solution: Transfer more of the risk to the insurance company. The trade here was to increase the deductible to $5,000 and use the premium savings to increase the amount of coverage for the structure. Francesca said she is fine with higher deductibles and writing what she feels are smaller checks.

Protecting Their Daily-Use Cars and Vehicle Collection

John's interest in our conversation really perked up as it migrated to their regular-use automobiles and the 11 collector cars that are his passion. I began by telling John, "The way the current coverage is set up for both your daily use and your collectors is like wearing a hospital gown. You know you have some coverage but you're just not sure how much of your behind is hanging out for the world to see." John got the gist of this analogy pretty quickly, but there were many items to cover up.

Problem: The automobile policy for the BMW and Range Rover included high limits of liability for bodily injury and property damage to third parties of $500,000, which was a good start. But the uninsured/underinsured motorist coverage was providing a limit of only $100,000.

Solution: Increase the uninsured motorist coverage to at least $500,000. I explained to John that this is money payable to you in the event you are involved in an incident with an uninsured/underinsured driver who is partially or fully at fault.

Problem: The $500 deductibles for the BMW and Range Rover are not consistent with Francesca and John's planning objectives.

Solution: Increase the deductibles on these two vehicles to $1,000 each, generating a premium savings. Then invest the premium savings toward increased coverage for the uninsured/underinsured motorist limit, plus other changes in their program.

Problem: Both the BMW and Range Rover are late-model high-value vehicles. Their current insurer would pay for these vehicles on the basis of market value. This could be a nightmare at claim time.

Solution: Obtain coverage that would pay on the basis of agreed value. In a way, this settles the loss before the claim. Francesca and John know they will receive the higher of either the market value of the car or the agreed value shown in the policy. Most insurance companies don't offer this coverage.

Problem: Their current insurer is notorious for repairing vehicles with after-market parts. When I pointed this out to John, he nearly hit the roof, the sign of a real auto enthusiast.

Solution: Work with an insurance company that is familiar with the high net worth marketplace and the vehicles they drive. Francesca and John now know their vehicles will be repaired with original equipment manufacturers' parts. In addition, Francesca and John can have the vehicle repaired at their choice of repair facilities, not one mandated by an insurance company.

With their daily-use cars now properly covered, I had to hit John where it really hurts—his auto collection. "John, I'm sorry, but the hospital gown still has your behind hanging out there for the world to enjoy. Let's talk about your eleven collector vehicles. I will keep it brief. Many of the items found here are similar to what I found with the BMW and Range Rover. There are some additional items, though. Let me show you."

Problem: So many cars, so many policies, so little coordination, and limits that went from high to low and back again—a few times. This left enormous self-insured gaps, especially with regard to attaching to the personal umbrella policy. Collectors tend to open up a new policy with varying liability limits each time they acquire a new vehicle.

Solution: Create one specialized policy with the 11 vehicles scheduled to the policy. The liability limits for bodily injury and property damage to third parties, along with the uninsured/underinsured motorist limits, would all be maximized and consistent to prevent any self-insured gap in attaching to the personal umbrella policy.

Problem: His insurance policies contained very restrictive language on collector vehicle usage. This is incompatible with John's love of driving in club rallies and long drives on the weekends.

Solution: Obtain antique and collector vehicle coverage that provides John with unlimited mileage and unrestrictive use of these fantastic automobiles.

In the event the car is damaged, John also has his choice of repair shops, agreed-value coverage with no deductible, and a claim department willing to work with restoration specialists. This was reassuring to John, who was concerned about being able to restore his vehicles to their original splendor in the event they were damaged.

Protecting Her Art Collection and Valuables

Over the last several years, Francesca has really become passionate about her art collection. She began with a desire to furnish her home with fine art. She then blossomed into a full-scale collector, focusing primarily on emerging artists. Soon, she found herself loaning the majority of her works to galleries and museums in the region, as a way to both support the artists and boost her return on investment.

Problem: Francesca made a habit of loaning pieces of her art collection without implementing risk management strategies to assure the safekeeping of these valuable works.

Solution: Help Francesca implement a risk management plan to follow prior to and during the time works are loaned to museums and galleries. This includes making sure museums have adequate safety measures and insurance. Another concern to address when loaning items to a museum is where the collection will be displayed. I also suggested to Francesca that I review the museum's insurance policy to make sure the collection will have adequate coverage.

Problem: Francesca has a great eye for acquiring interesting pieces of art. Her business and family schedule, though, has not allowed her the time to implement a strategy to manage her collection.

Solution: I helped Francesca choose an insurance company that caters specifically to the needs of high net worth clients—one that knows how to handle temporary fluctuations in the replacement cost of valuable articles. The best policies will pay market value up to 50 percent higher than the scheduled amount of coverage in case of loss. Francesca and I also agreed to annually review the inventory of valuable collections, and adjust coverage levels as needed.

Francesca must make sure items she acquires during the year are added to the insurance policy. The best insurance companies automatically provide coverage for newly acquired items, but they all require notice within a certain period of time, usually 30 to 90 days, depending on the item. In addition, we implemented a collection management strategy, using services offered by her new insurance company. This service will help her track the location of pieces, the date acquired, the last appraisal date, valuation at time of purchase, and the current insurance amount. Francesca admitted that implementing these strategies will help ease her worries about the safety of her collection.

Vermont—The Weekend Oasis

The rolling hills of the Green Mountains of Vermont beckon many people from the Metropolitan New York area to buy or build the country home of their dreams. Francesca bought a beautiful home loaded with New England charm, outside of Manchester, Vermont. This is when planning for Francesca and John became even more interesting. By purchasing several policies from a local agent in Vermont, their personal risk management and insurance program became fragmented. The first items we addressed were like those we found at their home in Old Brookville. It was time to get the rest of the Vermont exposure treated correctly.

Problem: One home policy in New York had $1,000,000 personal liability coverage and another home policy in Vermont had $300,000 personal liability coverage. Each policy could respond to an incident that happened on one premises or the other. What would happen if the incident occurs somewhere else, say at a house they rent in Colorado for a getaway with friends? Then which policy responds?

Solution: Add the Vermont home as a secondary home for personal liability to the policy covering the Old Brookville home. This assures a higher limit of personal liability and attachment to the personal umbrella liability policy without any gap in coverage. It also eliminates the question of which insurance company would pay in the case of a claim where either company could respond.

Problem: Too many cooks in the kitchen spoil the broth. The agent in Vermont was very good at servicing Francesca's needs. However, as I have seen happen many times before, this agent did not dig deeply enough or ask enough questions to make sure the policies he placed were correctly coordinated with the rest of the clients' insurance portfolio.

Solution: One agent will handle the entire risk management and insurance plan for Francesca. This ultimately provides several benefits to Francesca, including cost savings, one point of contact, elimination of coverage gaps, and consolidated paperwork coming from one insurance company on one billing statement.

Here are additional home exposures covered in the personal risk management plan:

Problem: Their growing stable of horses presents liabilities on several fronts.

Solution: Added equine liability insurance as separate coverage.

Problem: While on vacation in Vermont, they operate snowmobiles and ATVs off property, which is not covered by their homeowners policies.

Solution: Snowmobile and ATV policies are provided and schedules attached to the personal umbrella liability policy.

How Much Umbrella Liability Should I Have?

Francesca and John scratched their heads on this, as do many of my clients. To help them better understand their exposure, I walked them through the planning process discussed in Chapter 10:

1. Identify and analyze loss exposures.
2. Identify and select risk management techniques.
3. Implement chosen risk management techniques.
4. Monitor and measure the risk management program to seek improvements and adapt to changes.

Problem: Their current umbrella liability policy provided only $2,000,000 of additional protection. In addition, it was purchased through an insurance company not well suited for the high net worth family.

Solution: After a discussion, we all felt more comfortable with a personal umbrella limit of $15,000,000. This limit is more in line with their net exposed assets. The policy includes additional features, such as uninsured motorist protection of $5,000,000, protection for personal directors' and officers' liability as a director or officer at a not-for-profit organization, and choice of defense counsel.

Personal Staff Concerns

The full-time nanny who lives with Francesca and John provides an exposure that must be treated in different ways. Francesca and John felt just having a home insurance policy with personal liability coverage would be sufficient. I explained to them the best ways to transfer the risks associated with the nanny back to the insurance industry.

> **Problem:** The State of New York, and many other states, requires that workers compensation be provided to all domestic employees. This provides coverage for medical expenses and lost wages due to an injury that occurs during the course of employment. The State of New York, and many other states, also requires employers to provide short-term disability benefits coverage for employees. This provides coverage to the employee for an illness or injury that occurs away from the job. Childbirth is a common short-term disability claim for which employees are entitled to benefits.

> **Solution:** Policies for Workers Compensation and for short-term disability benefits were issued, naming Francesca and John as the insured as they are the employers of the Nanny.

> **Problem:** Poor recordkeeping and incomplete background checks during the hiring process. Francesca and John hired a nanny who was referred to them by a neighbor. She seemed to be very responsible and personable, and they offered her the job shortly after their first meeting. They did not ask for a resume, references, or an application for employment. Nor do John and Francesca have any sort of contract or employee handbook to outline the rules and expectations of employment.

> **Solution:** Help them set up a strategy to check background, and create an employee file and an employee handbook. Francesca and John should have a strategy to sever the relationship if necessary and their paperwork must be in good order to prevent an angry former employee from suing them for wrongful termination.

FRANCESCA'S DIRECTORSHIP

Recognized for her contributions to the art community, the local art museum enthusiastically invited her to serve on its board of directors. While she was aware that she was exposed to legal liabilities, she had assumed the organization's liability insurance had her covered.

> **Problem:** As with many of my clients who serve on nonprofit boards, Francesca was surprised to learn that the majority of claims reported by nonprofit organizations were for third-party injuries, but that the most expensive claims were for financial mismanagement, employment practices, errors and omissions, and sexual harassment. In other words, there is a lot of expensive liability exposure. Francesca's personal umbrella policy did not extend to all of the possible risks, leaving her vulnerable in certain circumstances.

> **Solution:** I recommended she purchase a separate nonprofit directors and officers (D&O) insurance add-on to their personal liability policy, which would pay on top of the organization's coverage. We also contacted the organization's insurance broker to ensure that its own coverage was adequate so there would be no gaps in coverage.

FINAL STRATEGIES FOR FRANCESCA AND JOHN

Having completed the first few steps of personal risk management planning, Francesca and John felt assured that most of the risks, of which they had been unaware, were now transferred to the insurance industry or contractually transferred to another party.

Additional transfer strategies we implemented include creating certificate of insurance templates for Francesca and John to use with contractors and other parties that provide services at their residences.

The appraisal services of an independent expert art appraisal and advisory firm were arranged to assist Francesca with the valuation and management of her growing art collection. The appraisal firm provided appraisals compliant with both Internal Revenue Service Guidelines and Uniform Standards of Professional Appraisal Service (USPAP) for the additional purposes of estate and tax planning, donation and using her art as collateral.

Francesca and John understood the need for coordination of their advisory team. A lunch meeting was arranged that included Francesca and John, their wealth advisor, trust and estate attorney, CPA, Pam the assistant, and me. The discussions at that meeting focused on the lives of Francesca and John with each advisor providing insight and expertise to help the other advisors manage their affairs for Francesca and John more effectively.

SUMMARY

As with most of my new clients, the personal risk management planning process at the next level was a revelation for Francesca and John; from exploring their lifestyle preferences and needs to identifying their exposures, to systematically implementing a deliberate plan to counter or transfer the risks, they have never felt more knowledgeable about the risks that pervade their daily lives. With access to an agency website with useful resources and a risk management guidebook, Francesca and John are still finding ways to reduce their exposures to risk.

Being the gracious people they are, they were not shy about admitting their ignorance of such critical matters. They quickly realized that risk management planning at the next level involves much more than generic insurance policies. Francesca and John also realize that it requires a trusting relationship with specialists who truly understand their unique situation. More important, with their newfound knowledge and a fully implemented plan, they have never felt more secure.

Conclusion

Most of us want to believe that we live in a safe community and that unfortunate events only happen to other people; but, being risk-adverse people, we at least take the essential step of insuring our houses, cars, and even our lives, because it is the responsible thing to do. However, things have a way of changing on the way to the *next level*. Houses get bigger, cars are more expensive, toys are bigger and more plentiful, and lifestyles are more lavish. As much as we would like to think that wealth can make life easier, the difficult and oft-ignored reality is that it can actually make life more complicated, because with wealth comes a commensurate amount of financial exposure with the potential to lose it all.

The problem for people arriving at the next level is that wealth has a tendency to mask the additional risks it creates. For some, it is the air of invincibility that comes with wealth that creates a false sense of security. For most, it is simply ignorance of the increased risks their new station in life presents. And there are those who recognize the risks but who have severely underestimated them, or overestimated the amount of protection their traditional insurance solutions provide. All of these people are my clients, and all arrived at the next level with hopes for a better life; but all of them were dangerously exposed, not realizing that one unfortunate event could seriously jeopardize their enjoyment of a good life.

The clients you met in this book—John, the $100 million entrepreneur who saw his business associate taken down with a $10 million lawsuit; Jared, the owner who found his newly remodeled 7,000-square-foot home buried under an avalanche of sewage; Robert, the multimillionaire political aspirant; Nick and Tatiana, the tango duo; my friend and retired investment manager, Steve; and, of course, Francesca and John—are all unique individuals. Yet, they all share a few things in common: They are all extremely bright, successful, humble, and financially astute.

More importantly, they all reached the next level of wealth without making the attitudinal transition necessary to see their lives differently. They're the same people they have always been, which made it all the more difficult for them to comprehend the notion that their wealth could present the kind of risks and dangers that couldn't be addressed with traditional insurance solutions. Given the opportunity to view their lives through the prism of their new reality (in the form of a comprehensive risk assessment), they now understand that with wealth comes greater responsibility to protect it, and that only through a comprehensive, well-coordinated personal risk management plan can they hope to live their vision of a good life with the peace-of-mind that wealth should bring.

IT'S EASIER THAN YOU THINK

Wherever you might have stood prior to reading this book—unaware, ignorant, in denial, or in a languid state of procrastination—its purpose is not only to demystify the world of personal risk management, but also to provide a meaningful guide for taking that critical first step.

Actually, you've already taken the critical first step by educating yourself on the realities of your situation:

- You now know the risks you face.
- You have a better idea of the breadth of your own financial exposure.
- You have been awakened to the fact that you are not alone in your personal risk management deficiencies.
- You know that it takes specialized solutions to address your unique and complex needs.
- You have a clear understanding of the risk management process.
- You know that the only thing preventing you from having greater peace of mind is not taking the next step, which will now be much easier after reading this book.

Your next step is to meet with a trusted advisor—your attorney, your wealth manager, or your business planning specialist—to voice your concerns and insist on a referral to an independent insurance broker who specializes in personal risk management. If they are unable to point you in the right direction, you can ask a trusted colleague or friend who has already engaged in the process for a referral. Using Chapter 11 as your guide, you or your trusted advisor should thoroughly vet prospective specialists for their background, experience, education, and access to carriers, as well as their stated process and their client profile. Be sure to ask for client references. When you find the right specialist, your wealth will no longer be exposed.

Sample Personal Lines Checklist

Personal Lines Exposure Checklist

Client Name _____   Date _____

Coverage	Has Coverage	Needs Coverage	Not Interested
Miscellaneous Policies			
Aircraft			
Excess flood insurance (over federal flood program maximum limits)			
Excess uninsured motorists BI on umbrella (if available)			
Flood insurance			
Golf cart			
Lead paint liability (landlord)			
Motorcycle			
Motorhome/mobile home			
Non-owned automobile			
Personal umbrella (excess liability coverage above primary policies)			
Snowmobile			
Watercraft (boat, yacht, jet-ski, trailers, etc.)			
Workers Compensation			
Other			
Homeowners Form: 3, 4, 5, or 6			
Coverage A—Dwelling $			
Coverage B—Other structures $			
Coverage C—Personal property $			
Coverage D—Loss of use $			
Coverage E—Liability $			
Coverage F—Medical payments $			

(continued)

Coverage	Has Coverage	Needs Coverage	Not Interested
Property Options			
Business personal property			
Condominium—Additions and alterations $			
Deductible options			
Earthquake (building and personal property)			
Food spoilage			
Guaranteed dwelling replacement cost			
Identity theft			
Inflation guard %			
Increases limits			
Money, coins, etc.			
Securities, tickets, stamps $			
Jewelry, fur, etc.—Theft			
Silverware, goldware—Theft			
Credit card, financial transfer card, forgery $			
Loss assessment—Increased limits $			
Mold remediation			
Ordinance of law coverage—Increased limits needed			
Other structures—increased dwelling limit needed			
Other structures—increased personal property limit needed			
Personal property replacement cost			
Personal property—Special coverage			
Scheduled property valuation (agreed value, actual cash value, etc.)			
Scheduled property:			
Bicycles			
Cameras			
Computers			
Fine arts			
Fine arts with breakage			
Furs			
Golf equipment			
Jewelry			
Jewelry in-vault			

Coverage	Has Coverage	Needs Coverage	Not Interested
Jewelry with pairs and sets			
Musical instruments			
Wine collection			
Other items (list here):			
Sewer, drain, or sump-pump backup			
Special coverage endorsement			
Special form—Coverage A			
Tenants—Building additions and alterations $			
Windstorm, hurricane deductible			
Other			
Personal Liability Options			
Home office/Business activities			
Incidental farming—Residence premises			
Owned farm elsewhere			
Personal injury			
Property rented to others			
Residence employees			
Watercraft (boat, yacht, jet-ski, trailers, etc.)			
Other			
Automobile			
Vehicle #1 (owned, leased, other)			
Vehicle #2 (owned, leased, other)			
Vehicle #3 (owned, leased, other)			
Vehicle #4 (owned, leased, other)			
Driver #1—			
Driver #2—			
Driver #3—			
Driver #4—			
Liability $			
PIP (basic)			
Extended/Additional			
Work loss exclusion $			
Coordination military			
Deductible: Name insured			
Name insured + Dep. rel.			
Medical payments			
Uninsured motorists bodily injury			
Stacked non-stacked lower limits			
Underinsured motorists bodily injury			
Stacked non-stacked lower limits			
Uninsured motorist property damage			
Comprehensive—Deductible $			

(continued)

Coverage	Has Coverage	Needs Coverage	Not Interested
Limited collision			
Collision—Deductible $			
Waiver of deductible			
Customized, electronic, sound equipment $			
Towing and labor			
Rental reimbursement per day/Total			
Out of territory (USA & Canada)			
Mexican automobile			
Other			
Life, Health, Disability			
Buy/Sell insurance			
Individual life insurance			
Individual disability insurance			
Last to die insurance			
Long-term care insurance			
Travel accident			
Other			

Coverage and Service Comparison

Specialized Insurance Providers versus Typical Insurance Providers

Homeowners

Coverage Feature	Specialized Homeowners Policy	Typical Homeowners Policy
Guaranteed replacement cost	Uncapped in most states	Capped at 125%–150% of coverage
Back-up of sewer and drains	Included; up to dwelling value	Unavailable or limited
Business property	Up to $25,000	Up to $5,000
Deductible options	Up to $100,000 available	Limited
Flexible limits	Flexibility to tailor limits for personal property and other structures	Unavailable or limited
Cash settlement option	Up to replacement cost if not rebuilding after a total loss	Unavailable
Primary flood	Available	Unavailable
Equipment breakdown	Available	Unavailable
Mold	$10,000 with options up to 100% of dwelling limit	Unavailable
Kidnap expenses	$100,000	Unavailable
Identity fraud restoration expenses, ATM robbery, and financial fraud, embezzlement, or forgery	Available	Unavailable or limited

(continued)

Homeowners

Coverage Feature	Specialized Homeowners Policy	Typical Homeowners Policy
Traumatic threat or event recovery/family security	Available	Unavailable
Green rebuilding expenses	Available	Unavailable
Waiver of deductible on losses over $50,000	Available	Unavailable
Replacement cost cash out option	Included	Unavailable
Lock replacement	Included; no deductible	Unavailable or limited
Food spoilage	Included	Unavailable or limited
Disability alterations	Alteration expenses to make home accessible for a family member who becomes permanently disabled due to a sudden and accidental event	Unavailable
Loss prevention devices following a claim	Included; up to $2,500 available	Unavailable

Complimentary Services

Natural catastrophe protection	Some specialized providers offer the services of a Wildfire Protection Unit and a Hurricane Protection Unit designed to maximize preparedness and lessen the impact of damage when it can't be avoided	No services available
Home valuation and loss prevention consultation	Included	Unavailable
Background checks	Available for private staff, financial advisors and tenants	Unavailable; can be purchased by third party vendor for a fee

Automobile

Coverage Feature	Specialized Auto Policy	Typical Auto Policy
Worldwide protection	Included	Typically U.S. and Canada only
Agreed value	Included	Unavailable
Lease/loan gap	Included	Typically unavailable
Collector vehicles	Available	Typically unavailable
Original manufacturer's parts	Included; when available	Unavailable
Vehicle lock replacement	Included	Unavailable
Rental car following a claim	Up to $12,500 with no per day limit	Up to $900 with a per day limit
New car replacement	Included	Optional; limited
Overnight expenses	Two nights for breakdowns more than 50 miles from home $1,500	Unavailable
Cash settlement	Available	Unavailable
Towing	Included	Optional
Personal property	Included; up to $2,500	Unavailable
Choice of repair facility	Included	Limited

Personal Excess Liability

Coverage Feature	Specialized Excess Liability Policy	Typical Excess Liability Policy
Limit of liability	Up to $100 million	Up to $5 million
Under/uninsured motorist limits	Up to $10 million	Up to $1 million
Choice of legal counsel	Available; choose from a roster of preeminent law firms	Unavailable; company assigns without client involvement
Personal attorney participation in defense	Included up to $10,000 (up to $100,000 available)	Unavailable
Employment practices liability insurance	Available; up to $2 million in limits with an additional $25,000 of coverage for public relations needs	Unavailable
Reputation damage	Up to $250,000 for fees to a public relations firm to protect your reputation	Unavailable

(continued)

Personal Excess Liability

Coverage Feature	Specialized Excess Liability Policy	Typical Excess Liability Policy
Family trust option	Damages resulting from duties performed as a trustee of a family trust	Unavailable
Not-for-profit board liability	Available; up to $1 million	Unavailable
Worldwide protection	Included	Unavailable
Personal Injury	Included	Unavailable
Medical payments	$10,000	$1,000
Identity fraud restoration expense	Available; up to $100,000	Unavailable
Incidental business at home	Included	Unavailable
Kidnap expense	Available; up to $250,000	Unavailable
Defense costs	Outside the policy limit	Inside of policy limit

Complimentary Services	Specialized Insurance Provider	Typical Insurance Provider
Background checks	Available for private staff, financial advisors, tenants and international staff	Unavailable

Private Collections

Coverage Feature	Specialized Insurance Provider	Typical Insurance Provider
Worldwide protection	Included	Typically unavailable
Articles of others	Included if this class is already covered on the policy; up to $1 million	Unavailable
Market appreciation	Included; up to 150% of market value	Unavailable; cost to repair or replace
Newly acquired property	Included for up to 90 days; up to 25% per class	Lesser amount of 25% per class or $10,000 included; limited
Damage from earthquake; windstorm and flood	Included	Included; limited
Coverage in transit and on exhibition	Included	Unavailable

Complimentary Services

Collection management and loss prevention consultation	Included	Unavailable

Watercraft/Yacht

Coverage Feature	Specialized Insurance Provider	Typical Insurance Provider
Worldwide protection	Ability to provide pre-defined or worldwide navigation based on specific cruising plans	Only United States and Canadian inland waters; limited coastal cruising
Value of vessel	Unlimited	Limited capacity for higher values
Comprehensive Protection and Indemnity (P&I)	Full P&I limit coverage (no sub-limits) for bodily injury, property damage, pollution, marine environmental damage	Sub-limits per person for bodily injury, per accident for bodily injury and per accident for property damage
Defense costs	In addition to the P&I limit	Included within the P&I limit
"All risk" coverage	Coverage for all risks, except those that are specifically excluded	Coverage subject to exclusions; may include named perils only
Deductibles	Waived for total loss or collisions with third party at-fault vessels or damage to navigational electronics due to lightning	Deductible applies for all losses to hull, contents and electronics

Other Specialized Products

Coverage Feature	Specialized Insurance Provider	Typical Insurance Provider
Private aircraft	Available	Unavailable
Excess flood	Available	Unavailable
Kidnap, ransom, and extortion	Available	Unavailable
Worker's compensation	Available	Unavailable
Worldwide travel protection	Available	Unavailable
Basic healthcare for private staff	Available	Unavailable
International properties	Available	Unavailable

Source: ACE Private Risk Services and AIG Private Client Group: Coverage comparisons versus standard policies.

Specialized Flood Insurance versus Standard Flood Insurance

Coverage	Specialized Policy	Standard Policy
Basement property	Covered within dwelling limit; not limited to specific items	Excluded except certain appliances for the function of the home
Other permanent structures	Within dwelling limit up to $250,000	Limited to 10% of the dwelling amount
Additional living expenses	Up to $250,000 for up to 1 year	Not covered
Repair costs required by ordinance or law	Up to $75,000	Not covered
Business property	Up to $25,000	Up to $2,500
Special limits	Included with no special limits for fine collectibles (jewelry, antiques, furs)	No more than $2,500 for any one loss
Property removal and safekeeping	No sub-limit	Up to $1,000
Secondary residences	Replacement cost on seasonal/secondary residences and contents	Actual cash value on seasonal/secondary residences and contents
Precautionary repairs	No sub-limit	Up to $1,000

Source: AIG Private Client Group/ACE Private Risk Services.

Ten Items to Include in Family Disaster Plan

1. Secure your home and take precautionary steps to eliminate hazards.
2. Keep fresh first aid kits and get family members trained in CPR.
3. Identify family meeting places and an outside family member or friend as a central contact.
4. Maintain a supply of fresh drinking water.
5. Maintain a supply of non-perishable foods.
6. Have emergency supplies ready (battery operated radio, first aid kit, toiletries, filtered masks, medicines).
7. Develop and share an emergency evacuation plan.
8. Store an emergency kit in your vehicle in the event of a disaster or being stranded in your vehicle.
9. Ask about and understand the procedures in the disaster plan at your work and at your children's school.
10. Keep you family disaster plan up to date and practice the steps in your plan so your family members understand what to do when disaster strikes.

Additional details can be found at:

WWW.III.ORG—Insurance Information Institute.
WWW.IRMI.COM—Insurance Risk Management Institute.

Breakdown of Audio and Video Recording Laws

How can you be sure if it's okay to record video or audio in certain circumstances? There are myriad laws that cover the video and audio recording of third parties. They differ by state as well as in the use of video versus audio. Here's the breakdown:

VIDEO RECORDING

Most video recordings are legal with or without consent.

There are very few laws that prohibit video recording of any kind, but there are laws in some areas dealing with *areas of expected privacy*. These include areas such as bathrooms, locker rooms, changing/dressing rooms, adult bedrooms, and other areas where a person should expect a high level of personal privacy.

The majority of the laws dealing with video recording privacy issues tend to allow surreptitious recording and monitoring of video activity under most circumstances without notification of any of the parties involved.

So far, the courts have allowed video recordings of nannies, elder-care employees, and other types of video recordings made with covert cameras without the subjects' consent.

AUDIO RECORDING

Most audio recordings without consent of one or all parties are illegal.

Recording audio is very different from video; there are definite federal and state laws prohibiting surreptitious recording and monitoring of audio conversations. These laws are taken very seriously by authorities and failure to abide by them could result in severe consequences.

There are two types of defined recording situations for audio recording. They are usually referred to as *one-party consent* and *two-party consent:*

- *One-party consent:* Only the person doing the recording has to give consent and does not have to notify the other party or parties that the conversation is being recorded.
- *Two-party consent:* The person recording the conversation must notify all of the other parties that the recording is taking place and they must consent to the recording.

Sixteen states require two-party consent and the rest require only one-party consent. The 16 states that require two-party consent are California, Connecticut, Delaware, Florida, Hawaii, Illinois, Kansas, Maryland, Massachusetts, Michigan, Montana, Nevada, New Hampshire, Pennsylvania, Utah, and Washington.

Laws change constantly. Please check your state's current laws before engaging in recording. *Always check with an attorney before recording to make sure it is legal where you live.*

Notes

1. National Flood Insurance Program, www.floodsmart.gov.
2. IRS Form 706, www.IRS.gov.
3. ACE Private Risk Services, "Wealth Risk: How High Net Worth Families Overpay to Be Underinsured" (March 2013).
4. "Rapaport Diamond Report" (2012).
5. IRS Publication 926, "Household Employer's Tax Guide," www.IRS.gov.
6. National Underwriter P&C, "Classic-Car Owners Face Sandy Heartbreak" (December 3–10, 2012).
7. Insurance.com (2012).
8. Non-Profit Insurance, http://goodworksinsurance.com/Site/142172544/NON_PROFITS_INSURANCE.asp.
9. "Why the Rich Fear Violence in the Streets," *Wall Street Journal* (June 6, 2011).
10. "Rich, Famous—and Vulnerable, Thanks to Identity Crisis," CBS Sportline.com.
11. Ace Private Risk Services, "Targeting the Rich: Liability Lawsuits and the Threat to Families with Emerging and Established Wealth" (March 2012).

Insurance Glossary

abandonment clause: A clause often contained in property insurance policies stating that the insured cannot abandon damaged property to the insurer and later demand to be reimbursed for its full value.

accident: A sudden and unexpected event, which occurs at a specific time and place. In easy-to-read policies, an accident is also defined as a loss, which occurs over a period of time.

actual cash value (ACV): The cost to replace an item of property at the time of loss, less an allowance for depreciation. Often used to determine amount of reimbursement for a loss (replacement cost–depreciation).

additional living expense: A property coverage included in dwelling and older homeowners contracts, designed to reimburse the insured for an increase in living expenses necessitated by loss to the dwelling. This indirect loss must be the result of direct loss by a covered peril.

aftermarket part: A vehicle replacement part manufactured by a company other than the vehicle maker. These parts are less expensive than the original equipment manufacturer (OEM) part. There is ongoing controversy as to whether aftermarket parts are equal to or inferior to OEM parts. Individual states have various rules and regulations regarding the use of aftermarket parts.

agent: The state-licensed professional who represents the insurance company in the sale and servicing of insurance. The direct link between the insurance company and the policyholder.

aggregate limit: A type of policy limit found in liability policies; limits coverage to a specified total amount for all losses occurring within the policy period.

agreed value coverage: An optional coverage written with property insurance policies. It waives the coinsurance clause and requires the insured to carry insurance equal to at least 80 percent of a signed statement of values filed with the company.

aleatory: A characteristic of insurance contracts, meaning a contract in which equal value is not given by both parties to the contract.

all risk insurance: Insurance protecting the insured from losses arising from perils other than those perils specifically excluded by name.

This contrasts with *named peril* insurance, which names the peril or perils insured against.

assumption of risk: A defense against liability based on the common law principle that a person who has been made aware of dangers beforehand assumes the risk and cannot attribute the loss to another.

attractive nuisance: A dangerous place or instrumentality attractive to children, like a swimming pool without a fence. The owner of an attractive nuisance has the legal duty of taking unusual care to guard children from it.

betterment: A reduction in an insurance claim payment arising out of the replacement of a partially worn part with a new part. An insurer applies betterment when a damaged vehicle part that has finite lifespan, such as a tire, is replaced by a new part. For example, if a new tire replaces a tire with 50 percent wear, the insurer will reduce the amount paid for the new tire by 50 percent.

binder: An oral or written statement providing immediate insurance protection, valid for a specified period. Designed to provide temporary coverage until a policy can be issued or denied.

Blanket insurance: Insurance where a single amount of insurance applies to two or more coverage items.

bodily injury: Usually defined to include physical harm, sickness, disease, or death resulting from any of these.

broker: An individual who represents the prospect, instead of the insurance company, in the insurance transaction. Frequently involved in the placement of very large or unusual risks.

casualty insurance: A line of insurance that historically has included a wide variety of unrelated coverages. One important coverage in the casualty line is liability. Casualty also includes aviation, auto, boiler and machinery, crime, Workers Comp, and surety bonds.

civil liability: Liability involving actions brought by persons against others for money damages or other relief such as injunctions, accounts, and specific performance.

claimant: One who makes a liability claim against another person's insurance policy.

coinsurance clause: A clause that requires an insured to pay part of a loss if the coverage provided under the policy limits is less than a specified percentage of the value of the property at the time of loss.

collision: A type of physical damage insurance that covers loss due to the insured object striking another object. Collision may also include upset of the insured object.

commercial lines: Insurance designed for businesses, institutions, or organizations.

common law: A body of principles and rules of action arising from usages and customs or from judgments of courts that recognize, affirm, and enforce custom. Common law is unwritten in that it has never been enacted into statute law.

compensatory damages: Monetary awards that compensate an injured party only for losses that were actually sustained. Compensatory damages include special damages and general damages.

comprehensive coverage: In automobile insurance, a broad physical damage coverage that covers all property losses except collision and those perils or property that are specifically excluded. Comprehensive coverage covers such items as theft, vandalism, and storm damage.

concealment: The withholding of a material fact from the insurance company. May void the policy.

consideration: A characteristic of a legal contract: the thing of value exchanged for the performance promised in the contract. In insurance, the policy premium is the consideration.

contingent liability: Liability that an insured or business incurs because of the actions of others (i.e., family or employees). Also called *vicarious liability*.

debris removal: A coverage provided in many property contracts that reimburses the insured for expenses involved in removing debris produced by a loss from a peril insured against.

declarations: The section of an insurance contract that clarifies who is insured, what property or risk is covered, when and where coverage is effective, and how much coverage applies.

deductible: Usually, a dollar amount the insured must pay on each loss to which the deductible applies. The insurance company pays the remainder of each covered loss up to the policy limits.

degree of care: Extent of duty owed by one person to another.

depreciation: A decrease or loss in value because of wear, age, or other cause. In accounting, an allowance made for this loss.

direct loss: Loss that is a direct result of a peril. Also includes loss due to efforts to end the peril or to unavoidable exposure following a peril.

due care: The degree of care that is required to protect others from unreasonable chance of harm; the standard of conduct a "reasonably prudent" person would observe in a given situation.

dwelling policy: Policy designed to provide property coverage to individuals and families. Covers dwellings, other structures, personal property, and fair rental value. Does not require owner-occupancy for eligibility.

endorsement: A document that is attached to the policy and modifies or changes the original policy in some way.

errors and omissions: A professional liability coverage that protects the insured against liability for committing an error or omission in performance of professional duties. An insurance agent would carry such coverage.

excess insurance: Coverage that applies only after the limits of the primary insurance have been exhausted. See: *primary insurance.*

exclusions: The section of the insurance policy that lists property, perils, persons, or situations that are not covered under the policy.

face value: The total amount or principal amount of insurance provided by an insurance policy. The term derives from the fact that the amount of insurance is usually indicated on the first page or "face" of the policy.

financial responsibility laws: Each state has its own laws that require owners or operators of autos to provide evidence that they have the funds to pay for automobile losses for which they might become liable. Insurance is the usual method for providing this evidence to the state. Each state has its own minimum requirements.

floater: An insurance contract that applies to property wherever it is moved, rather than applying only at a fixed location.

flood insurance: Insurance designed to reimburse property owners for loss due to flood or to flood-related erosion. Administered through the Federal Emergency Management Agency, but marketed through independent agents.

general damages: Damages that are awarded in an attempt to compensate for such things as pain, suffering, humiliation, embarrassment, and disfigurement.

gross negligence: Conduct that fails to meet even the minimum standard of care that persons with common sense would take for their own safety and that of their property. Conduct showing total disregard for the safety of others—reckless, wanton, and willful misconduct.

hazard: Something that increases the chance of loss. For instance, faulty wiring is a hazard because it increases the chance of a fire loss.

homeowners policy: A personal multiple-line contract incorporating both property and liability coverages. Six different policies provide varying degrees of protection.

hull insurance: In ocean marine and aviation insurance, insurance against physical damage to a plane or ship.

implied warranties: Warranties that are not written into the policy, but have become part of policy by custom.

incurred losses: Losses or claims that the insurance company has paid or for which it has become liable; or paid losses plus reserves for a certain period, minus unpaid reserves at the end of the previous period.

indemnification: A principal of insurance that provides that when a loss occurs, the insured should be restored to the approximate financial condition occupied before the loss occurred, no better, no worse. An insurance company can indemnify an individual through the replacement or repair or payment of value of a loss. Not to be confused with legal damages, which frequently go beyond indemnity.

inland marine insurance: A form of insurance originally designed as an extension of marine coverage to insure transportation of goods over land. Today, it covers, in addition to goods in transit, a variety of portable property.

insurable interest: Any actual, lawful, and substantial economic interest in the safety or preservation of the subject of the insurance from loss, destruction, or pecuniary damage or impairment. Relationship or condition such that loss or destruction of life or property would cause a financial loss. A claim may be paid only when an insurable interest exists.

insurance: A contract or device for transferring risk from a person, business, or organization to an insurance company that agrees, in exchange for a premium, to pay for losses through an accumulation of premiums.

insuring agreement: The section of an insurance policy that states which losses will be indemnified, what property is covered, and which perils are insured against.

limits of liability: The maximum amount of insurance the insurance company will pay for a particular loss, or for a loss during a period of time; 15/30/10 would mean $15,000 maximum limit per person for bodily injury for any one occurrence, $30,000 maximum total paid for bodily injuries per occurrence, and $10,000 maximum per occurrence for property damages.

loss: In insurance, the term means the amount the insurer is required to pay because of a happening against which it has insured. Also, a happening that causes the company to pay. Also refers to the overall financial result of some operation, as opposed to *profit*. The basis for a claim for indemnity or damage under the terms of an insurance policy. Any diminution of quality, quantity, or value of property.

loss of consortium: Involves actions to recover for injury to familial relationships, especially when negligently inflicted. A husband may have a monetary claim for loss of consortium after an accident involving his wife for the period of time when the wife is disabled and/or unable to provide him with physical comforts, including sexual relations.

loss-of-use coverage: Under the homeowners contract, covers the insured's increased cost of living after loss and rental value of any portion of the dwelling that is rented out.

malpractice insurance: A form of professional liability insurance used to insure professionals, including physicians, dentists, and druggists, against their liability for professional misconduct or lack of ordinary skill.

market value: The amount that a seller may expect to obtain for merchandise, services, or securities in the open market. An insurance company may pay you the market value of your automobile if it was declared a total loss from a covered peril.

material misrepresentation: To make written or verbal statements that are untrue or misleading, either intentionally or unintentionally. For instance, if you exclude a resident driver of your household on the application of insurance, this may be grounds for invalidating the insurance contract since the insurance company did not have the opportunity to rate this driver when determining the amount of premiums to charge.

mitigation of damages: A plaintiff is responsible for any loss that occurs as a result of his or her own lack of care following an accident. An individual must do his or her best to mitigate (lessen) the damages resulting from an accident.

moral hazard: The hazard present in an insuring situation if the insured purposely creates a loss to later collect from the insurance company.

morale hazard: The hazard present in an insuring situation if the insured, through carelessness or as a result of his or her own irresponsible action, creates a loss.

named non-owner coverage: An endorsement that can be added to the personal auto policy to provide coverage for a named individual who does not own an auto while the insured is operating autos owned by others.

named peril policy: Insurance contract that insures only against perils named in the policy.

negligence: Failure to do what a reasonably prudent individual would ordinarily do under the circumstances of a particular case, or doing what a prudent person would not have done. The failure to exercise that degree of care that the law requires to protect others from an unreasonable risk of harm. Negligence may involve acts of omission, commission, or both. Lack of due care. Breach of duty owed.

no-fault insurance: A form of automobile insurance mandated by law in many states whereby an insurance company reimburses its insured for auto losses, regardless of fault, and without resort to subrogation. This is usually related to the medical bills of the insured paid under their personal injury protection (PIP) coverage.

occurrence: Coverage on an *occurrence* basis is generally considered to differ from coverage on an *accident* basis in that *occurrence* connotes gradual or accumulative damages without regard to exact time or place, whereas *accident* refers to instantaneous damage, identifiable as to time and place. In other words, *occurrence* may be defined as an event, or repeated exposure to conditions, that unexpectedly causes injury during the policy period.

open perils: See: *all risk.*

peril: Refers to the causes of possible loss, such as fire, windstorm, explosion, etc.

personal articles floater: Personal inland marine insurance that provides all risk coverage on nine optional classes of personal property: jewelry, furs, cameras, musical instruments, silverware, golf equipment, fine arts, stamp collections, and coin collections.

power of attorney: The written instrument by which the authority of one person to act in the place and stead of another as his or her attorney in fact is set forth.

primary insurance: When two or more coverages or policies apply to the same loss, the one that pays first, up to its limits of liability or the amount of the loss, whichever is less. See: *excess insurance.*

proof of loss: A statement signed by the policyholder making formal claim against the company for damage to or loss of the property insured.

pro-rata: A method of handling insurance when more than one policy applies to a loss. Each policy covers a portion of the loss in proportion to the relationship its limit of liability bears to the total limit of liability under all applicable policies.

punitive damages: Damages awarded to punish the wrongdoer for antisocial actions, rather than simply reimbursing the plaintiff for the loss. Punitive damages are awarded when the injury is intended, or involves a wrong more flagrant than negligence.

"reasonable person": A pattern of behavior used as a basis for defining negligent conduct. One is required to act as though he or she has the physical attributes of the person actually involved in the case, as well as to exercise a certain degree of mental capacity—that of the average person of similar age and experience. Persons holding themselves out as having superior skills, knowledge, or intelligence also have a special standard of conduct imposed on them, which is higher than the one imposed on the average person.

rental value: An indirect property coverage available under dwelling and homeowners policies and also available with certain commercial contracts that reimburses the insured for rents lost when rented property is damaged by a peril insured against.

replacement cost endorsement: An endorsement that can provide replacement cost coverage for personal property when added to the Homeowners Special Form (HO-3).

salvage: The property in which an insurance company secures an ownership interest as a result of paying a claim for total loss or damage based on the true value of the property in its undamaged state or before the loss occurred.

special damages: Damages that compensate for direct and specific expenses that are involved in a loss, including property damage, medical bills, loss of use, rental expenses, and lost wages. Special damages do not include compensation for inconvenience or pain and suffering.

strict liability: Refers to the direct responsibility for damages resulting from a deliberate action that is potentially hazardous.

total loss: Loss to the insured of the entire value of goods or other property by destruction, damage, or deprivation. Also, loss entailing the payment of the face amount of an insurance contract. Also, property damages to the extent that the cost of repairs exceeds the market value less the salvage value.

umbrella liability policy: Provides broad coverage for an insured's liability over and above liability covered by underlying contracts or retention limits. Can be personal or commercial.

underinsured motorist coverage: A coverage that reimburses the insured for the difference between the actual damages sustained by the insured for bodily injury and the amount of liability insurance that meets the state's minimum financial requirements carried by the driver who was at fault, up to the limits of the insured's underinsured motorist coverage.

underwriting: The insurance function that researches and evaluates insurance applications to decide which are acceptable to the company as insureds.

uninsured motorist coverage: Automobile coverage designed to provide protection for the insured should he or she be included in an accident in which the driver at fault has no insurance to cover the loss.

vicarious liability: Negligence that is not directly attributable to the person claimed against, but that is the negligence of another for whom the person claimed against is in some way responsible. Also known as *imputed liability.*

waiver: The relinquishment of a right, either expressly or by implication. Express waiver is made voluntarily. In insurance matters, the policy may be reformed by endorsement or otherwise amended. Implied waiver may result from misleading actions or neglect on the part of the claim representative. A claim representative is not privileged in this area and must avoid all acts of waiver except those that the insurer has instructed the claim representative to perform.

workers Compensation insurance: Insurance that covers an employer's obligations under Workers Compensation laws, and that makes the employer responsible for stated damages in the event of a work-related injury or illness. Workers Compensation coverage also includes separate coverage for employers liability.

wrongful death: Action on account of injuries that result in death before a claim for them was compromised or reduced to judgment. The death is judged to be needless, unjust, reckless, and unfair.

Useful Websites for Personal Risk Management and Insurance Information

WWW.IRMI.COM—International Risk Management Institute

WWW.III.ORG—Insurance Information Institute

WWW.FEMA.GOV—Federal Emergency Management Agency

WWW.ACEGROUP.COM—ACE Private Risk Services

WWW.AIGPRIVATECLIENT.COM—AIG Private Client Group

WWW.CHUBB.COM—Chubb Personal Insurance

WWW.FFIC.COM—Fireman's Fund Insurance Company

About the Author

Brian Flood, CPCU®, ARM™, has spent more than 20 years in commercial risk management and risk transfer, working with midsized organizations, family offices, successful entrepreneurs, executives, athletes, and other high-profile individuals to implement risk reduction strategies. Utilizing a highly personalized approach to personal risk management, Brian is highly regarded for developing creative risk management solutions and concepts unique to each individual or organization.

As vice president of the Flood Group, based in New York, Brian leads a team of both personal and commercial lines specialists to provide a complete suite of risk management services and products to a clientele that spans the country. A major thrust of the Flood Group's outreach to their clients is education because they have found that effective personal risk management begins with knowledge.

To that end, Brian, an avid writer himself, decided to write the book he has long been looking for but could never find as recommended reading for his clients—one that presents personal risk management concepts with clarity and appeal for busy high-net-worth individuals and their advisors.

When he's not working with clients to protect their lifestyles and businesses, Brian enjoys spending time with his true passion—his wife, Regina, and three children, Francesca, Andrew, and Peter John (PJ). A sports enthusiast, he splits his free time between coaching his kids' sports teams, golfing, and skiing. Brian is also actively involved with Rotary Club and Knights of Columbus.

Brian earned a BBA in management from Hofstra University and has earned industry designations as a Chartered Property Casualty Underwriter (CPCU) and Associate Risk Management (ARM). He holds licenses for Property & Casualty and Life, Accident & Disability.

Index